APL

AN INTRODUCTION

Hayden Computer Programming Series

BASICS OF DIGITAL COMPUTER PROGRAMMING (Second Ed.)
John S. Murphy

BASIC BASIC: An Introduction to Computer Programming in BASIC Language (Second Ed.)
James S. Coan

ADVANCED BASIC: Applications and Problems
James S. Coan

DISCOVERING BASIC: A Problem Solving Approach
Robert E. Smith

PROGRAMMING PROVERBS
Henry F. Ledgard

PROGRAMMING PROVERBS FOR FORTRAN PROGRAMMERS
Henry F. Ledgard

FORTRAN WITH STYLE: Programming Proverbs
Henry F. Ledgard and Louis J. Chmura

COBOL WITH STYLE: Programming Proverbs
Louis J. Chmura and Henry F. Ledgard

BASIC WITH STYLE: Programming Proverbs
Paul A. Nagin and Henry F. Ledgard

PASCAL WITH STYLE: Programming Proverbs
Henry F. Ledgard and Paul A. Nagin

FORTRAN FUNDAMENTALS: A Short Course
Jack Steingraber

THE BASIC WORKBOOK: Creative Techniques for Beginning Programmers
Kenneth E. Schoman, Jr.

BASIC FROM THE GROUND UP
David E. Simon

APL: AN INTRODUCTION
Howard A. Peelle

Z-80 AND 8080 ASSEMBLY LANGUAGE PROGRAMMING
Kathe Spracklen

```
                APLAPLAPL                 APLAPLAPLAPLAPLAPLAPLAPLAPL  APLAPLAPLAPLAPL
               APLAPLAPLAP                APLAPLAPLAPLAPLAPLAPLAPLAPLA APLAPLAPLAPLAPL
              APLAPLAPLAPLA               APLAPLAPLAPLAPLAPLAPLAPLAPLAPAPLAPLAPLAPLAPL
             APLAPLAPLAPLAPL                 APLAPLAPL          APLAPLAPL  APLAPLAPL
            APLAPLAP APLAPLAP                APLAPLAPL          APLAPLAPL  APLAPLAPL
           APLAPLAP   APLAPLAP               APLAPLAPL          APLAPLAPL  APLAPLAPL
          APLAPLAP     APLAPLAP              APLAPLAPL          APLAPLAPL  APLAPLAPL
         APLAPLAP       APLAPLAP             APLAPLAPL          APLAPLAPL  APLAPLAPL
        APLAPLAP         APLAPLAP            APLAPLAPL          APLAPLAPL  APLAPLAPL
       APLAPLAP           APLAPLAP           APLAPLAPL          APLAPLAPL  APLAPLAPL
      APLAPLAP             APLAPLAP          APLAPLAPL          APLAPLAPL  APLAPLAPL
     APLAPLAP               APLAPLAP         APLAPLAPL          APLAPLAPL  APLAPLAPL
    APLAPLAP                 APLAPLAP        APLAPLAPL          APLAPLAPL  APLAPLAPL
   APLAPLAPLAPLAPLAPLAPLAPLAPLAPLAPLAP       APLAPLAPLAPLAPLAPLAPLAPLAPL   APLAPLAPL
  APLAPLAPLAPLAPLAPLAPLAPLAPLAPLAPLAPLA      APLAPLAPLAPLAPLAPLAPLAPLAP    APLAPLAPL
 APLAPLAPLAPLAPLAPLAPLAPLAPLAPLAPLAPLAPL     APLAPLAPLAPLAPLAPLAPLAPLA     APLAPLAPL
 APLAPLAP                       APLAPLAP     APLAPLAPL                     APLAPLAPL          APLA
APLAPLAP                         APLAPLAP    APLAPLAPL                     APLAPLAPL         APLAP
APLAPLAP                          APLAPLAP   APLAPLAPL                     APLAPLAPL        APLAPL
APLAPLAPLAPLAPL               APLAPLAPLAPLAPLAPLAPLAPLAPLA              APLAPLAPLAPLAPLAPLAPLAPLAPLAPL
APLAPLAPLAPLAPL               APLAPLAPLAPLAPLAPLAPLAPLAPLA              APLAPLAPLAPLAPLAPLAPLAPLAPLAPL

                                                                  APLAPLAPL
                                                                   APLAPLAPL
                                                                    APLAPLAPL
                                                                     APLAPLAPL
                                                                      APLAPLAPL
                                                                       APLAPLAPL
                                                                        APLAPLAPL
                                                                         APLAPLAPL
                                                                          APLAPLAPL
LAPLAPLAPLAPLAPLAPLAPLAPLAPLAPLAPLAPLAPLAPLAPLAPLAPLAPLAPLAPLAPLAPLAPLAPLAPLAPLAPL
LAPLAPLAPLAPLAPLAPLAPLAPLAPLAPLAPLAPLAPLAPLAPLAPLAPLAPLAPLAPLAPLAPLAPLAPLAPLAPLAPLA
LAPLAPLAPLAPLAPLAPLAPLAPLAPLAPLAPLAPLAPLAPLAPLAPLAPLAPLAPLAPLAPLAPLAPLAPLAPLAPLAPL
                                                                          APLAPLAPL
                                                                         APLAPLAPL
                                                                        APLAPLAPL
                                                                       APLAPLAPL
                                                                      APLAPLAPL
                                                                     APLAPLAPL
                                                                    APLAPLAPL
                                                                   APLAPLAPL
                                                                  APLAPLAPL
```

AN INTRODUCTION

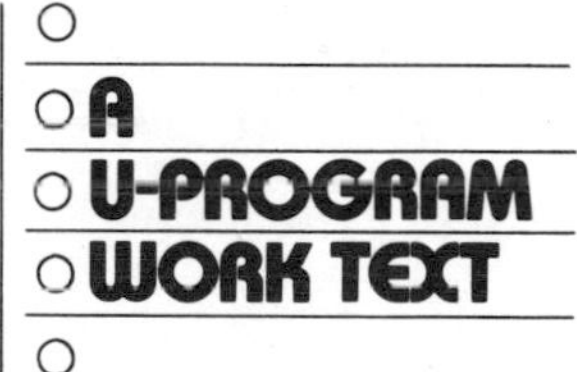

HOWARD A. PEELLE

University of Massachusetts
Amherst, Massachusetts

HAYDEN BOOK COMPANY, INC.
Rochelle Park, New Jersey

ISBN 0-8104-5122-0
Library of Congress Catalog Card Number 78-58616

Originally published for limited distribution as *APL/360 U-Programs.*

Printed in the United States of America

3	4	5	6	7	8	9	PRINTING
80	81	82	83	84	85	86	YEAR

PREFACE

Greetings! *APL: An Introduction* provides a set of *self-teaching* materials which provide an informal introduction to APL.* They are called "U-Programs" based on the belief that you will learn APL best if *you* program it yourself.

The APL U-Programs are designed for students at secondary and college levels who have a penchant for experimentation. Specifically, the materials may be used in the following ways:

1. Problem-Solving Exercises: Begin by observing examples of how APL functions and commands are used. Some examples show the computer's results, others (marked with an arrow ——→ in the margin) have the computer's display omitted and are exercises for you to do. Answers are provided in the Appendix. (Note that this does *not* require access to a computer; if one is available, it can be used to enter problems, observe results, and check answers.)

2. Experimentation and Exploration: Using the problems (from 1.) as samples, explore the nature of APL functions and commands by conducting "experiments" on the computer. For instance, an experiment might involve systematically varying different values with the same function, or trying different functions or combinations of functions.

3. Formalization and Generalization: Using the results of experimentation (from 2.) as an intuitive basis, then formally express—either in words (to a human instructor) or in a program definition (to the computer)—general rules for describing the behavior of an APL function. Such "simulations" and other programs may be written similarly to apply APL for your own purposes.

In all of these ways, the user of APL U-Programs is encouraged to use a "heuristic" approach to learning APL. That is, by examining patterns in the examples shown and from results of experiments conducted, the student may make reasonable conjectures about the nature of the APL language. These conjectures may be confirmed by subsequent experience or by an instructor or a manual.

---

*APL is *A Programming Language*, which was developed by Kenneth E. Iverson of IBM Corporation. Originally conceived as a unifying mathematical notation in the late 1950s and early 1960s, APL has since been implemented on a variety of computing systems and has been used successfully in business, scientific research, and education. For a list of APL publications, write: APL Press, Box 378, Pleasantville, N.Y. 10570.

The APL U-Programs are organized into nine units—each with a title page/table of contents and review. The learning progression is designed to be sequential but may be altered by skipping forward or backward at the student's discretion. Annotations in the right-hand margin are intended as supplementary explanation and may be overlooked by the independent-minded student.

Beginning with U-Program 1, APL tools for problem-solving are presented, and soon thereafter sample programs are demonstrated. Each of the U-Programs assumes a clear workspace, i.e., you enter expressions on an empty slate. APL expressions are indented 6 spaces, and the computer's response is shown at the left margin. Some expressions on the page are simply examples to be observed. Other expressions are exercises for the student to do (here the computer's response has been omitted and an arrow ⟶ shown instead). Additionally, some expressions are marked "challenge" for those who wish to stretch their understanding.

At any rate, *enjoy* APL.

HOWARD A. PEELLE

Amherst, Mass.

CONTENTS

ABOUT APL SYSTEMS

The version of APL used in this book corresponds closely to the standard IBM program product, as implemented on the IBM 360 and 370 series time-sharing systems and the IBM 5100 desk-top computer. Other versions of APL, such as APLUM (APL at the University of Massachusetts) implemented on a CDC CYBER 74, differ slightly and would affect the following topics in this book:

	page
Significant Digits	3
Attention Key	56
E Notation	59
Deleting Lines in a Program	61
Trace Command	64

Note also that the user is expected to arrange access to an APL computing system and, therefore, that this book does not describe equipment, sign-on procedures, or any aspects pertaining to interaction with a particular machine. Rather, it assumes that one is ready to study the APL language, per se.

APL KEYBOARD

U-Program 1

COMMAND EXECUTION

Contents

You type this

```
      'HELLO'
HELLO
```

The computer responds here

```
      'THESE ARE EXAMPLES OF APL EXPRESSIONS'
THESE ARE EXAMPLES OF APL EXPRESSIONS
```

Whatever you type between two quote marks is printed out

You write the answer here (As if you were the computer) →

```
      'WITH SOME FOR YOU TO DO'

      2 + 5
7
```

Examples of the arithmetic functions + - × ÷

```
      9 - 6
3

      3 × 4
12

      100 ÷ 5
20
```

You Do These

```
      4 + 8
→

      7 - 3
→

      5 × 20
→

      100 ÷ 4
→
```

```
    3.6 + 1.2
4.8
```

Decimal numbers are written in the normal way

```
    2.5 + 7.1
→
```

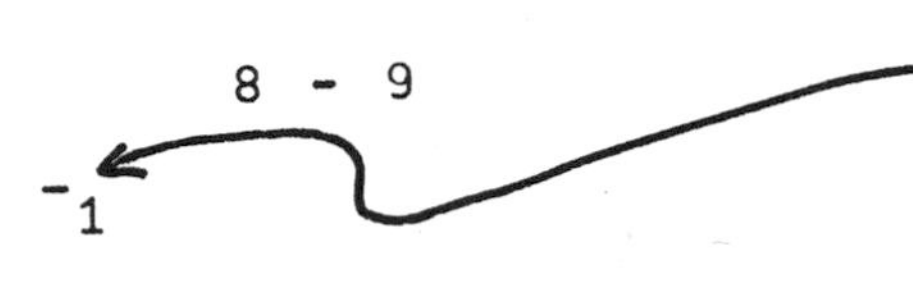

```
    8 - 9
¯1
```

the symbol for negative numbers (above the 2 on the keyboard) is different from the symbol for subtraction (above the +)

```
    4 - 7
→

    6 × 2.00
12
```

12 is equivalent to 12.00

```
    3.0 × 5
→

    100 ÷ 6
16.66666667
```

10 significant digits are printed

```
    100 ÷ 3
→
```

ERROR REPORTS

```
    100 ÷
SYNTAX ERROR
    100÷
       ^
```

The computer reports an error-- indicating that for proper syntax some number must follow ÷

(^ points to the function nearest the error)

No harm has been done.

You may continue.

```
      A ← 13
      A
13
      B ← 10
      B
10
```

Command to store some value and give it a name (Here 13 is the value; A is the name)

type A and the computer prints the value of A

This can be read as "B is assigned to be 10"

```
      A + B
23
```

You can use functions with named values.

```
      A - B
→
      A × B
→
```

(the value of A) times (the value of B)

```
      A ÷ B
1.3
```

```
      B × C
VALUE ERROR
      B×C
        ^
```

Here the computer reports an error indicating that C does not (yet) have a value. If you do B←10 first, C←5 then B×C 50 is OK.

REASSIGNMENT AND COUNTERS

```
      YEAR ← 1974
      YEAR ← 2001
      YEAR
2001
```

Several letters may be used for a name, like YEAR (Numbers and underscore _ and Δ also may be used in names; but names cannot have spaces nor begin with a number.)

The value of a name is determined by the latest assignment.

```
      COUNTER ← 1
      COUNTER
1
```

COUNTER is 1

```
      COUNTER ← COUNTER + 1
      COUNTER
2
```

COUNTER becomes 1 plus the old value of COUNTER

```
      COUNTER ← COUNTER + 1
      COUNTER
3
```

COUNTER is increased by 1 again

```
      COUNTER ← COUNTER + 1
      COUNTER
→
```

COUNTER is increased by 1 to become ?

```
      COUNTER ← COUNTER + 1
      COUNTER
→
```

What is the value of COUNTER now?

```
      YEAR
→
```

A name keeps its value (until it is re-assigned)

```
      SET ← 2
      SET
2
```

SET is initially assigned 2

```
      SET ← SET , 3
      SET
2 3
```

SET is reassigned. It becomes the value of SET with 3 chained on the end
(, chains values together)

```
      SET ← SET , 5
      SET
2 3 5
```

SET is reassigned to be 2 3 with 5 chained on the end

```
      SET ← SET , 7
      SET
→
```

SET is 2 3 5 with 7 chained on

```
      SET ← SET , 11
      SET
2 3 5 7 11
```

SET is 2 3 5 7 , 11

SET is now a set of numbers (called a "vector") and can be treated as a single entity.

For example,

```
      SET + 1
3 4 6 8 12
```

1 is added to each element of SET

```
      SET - 1
→
```

(2-1), (3-1), (5-1), (7-1)

```
      SET × 2
→
```

2 times each element of SET

```
      SET ← 2 3 5 7 11
      SIX ← 6 6 6 6 6
```

Assigning two vectors (with spaces between the numbers)

```
      SET × SIX
12 18 30 42 66
```

Element-by-element multiplication

```
      SET + SIX
→
```

(2+6), (3+6), (5+6), (7+6), (11+6)

```
      SET + 6
8 9 11 13 17
```

(An equivalent way of adding 6)

```
      SET , SIX
2 3 5 7 11 6 6 6 6 6
```

, chains the values together

```
      SET , 6
→
```

```
    V ← 2 3 5 7 11
    W ← 4 0 1 5 3
```
V and W are assigned values (Notice that each vector has 5 values)

```
    V + W
6 3 6 12 14
```
Element-by-element addition (This is "parallel processing")

```
    V - W
¯2 3 4 2 8
```
Element-by-element subtraction

```
    V × W
→
```
Multiply the first element in V times the first in W
then " second " " second "
then " third " " third "
then " fourth " " fourth "
then " fifth " " fifth "

```
    W × V
→
```
Element-by-element multiplication

```
    V , W
→
```
chain the values together

```
    W , V
→
```
chain the values together (W followed by V)

CATENATION ,

, is the "catenation" function. You have already seen it used with numbers (page 6)
The catenation function can be used with literal data too:

```
      D ← '*'                D is assigned the literal *
      D
*

      D , D                  , chains the value of D together
**                             with itself

      D , D , D , D
→


      E ← '∆'
      S ← '∆*∆'              More assignments
      I ← 'oo'
      G ← '∆'
      N ← 'o*'


      D , E , S , I , G , N
*∆∆*∆oo∆o*                   This is a literal vector

      D , E , S , I , G , N , S
→                            chain the symbols
                             together (in the order shown)
```

Storing letters (literals) in names

```
    E ← 'HINGT'

    G ← 'WAS'

    O ← 'ON'

    G , E , O
WASHINGTON
```

```
    A ← 'ABRA'

    L ← 'CAD'

    A , L , A
```

→

Note:
These are "overstrike" symbols
(Type ' backspace .)

```
    H ← 'SE YOU, RE'

    O ← 'D BAR'

    T ← 'ON!!!'

    S ← 'CUR'

    S , H , O , T
```

→

The Equals Function

```
      5 = 5
1
      4 = 6
0
      6 = 4
0
      ¯7.8 = ¯7.800
1
      8 = 11
→
      12 = 12
→
      5 3 5 7 5 3 5 5 = 5
1 0 1 0 1 0 1 1
```

Does 5 equal 5?
1 means "yes" (true)

0 means "no" (false)

Not true

True

For you to do

= with a vector

5 is compared with each element of the vector

1s result where there are 5s and 0s result everywhere else

The Less-Than Function

```
      3 < 5
1
```

Is 3 less than 5?
1 (true)

```
      8 7 6 5 4 < 5
0 0 0 0 1
```

Is 8 7 6 5 4 less than 5? 0 (false) 0 (false) 0 (false) 0 (false) 1 (true)

The Less-Than or Equal Function

```
      8 7 6 5 4 ≤ 5
0 0 0 1 1
```

The Greater-Than Function

```
      8 7 6 5 4 > 5
1 1 1 0 0
```

The Greater-Than or Equal Function

```
      8 7 6 5 4 ≥ 5
1 1 1 1 0
```

```
      V ← 1 5 4 ¯2 5 0 9
      V < 5
→

      V ≤ 5
→

      V > 5
→

      V ≥ 5
→
```

Answer 1 if true
and 0 if false

The Not-Equals Function

```
      V ≠ 5
1 0 1 1 0 1 1
```

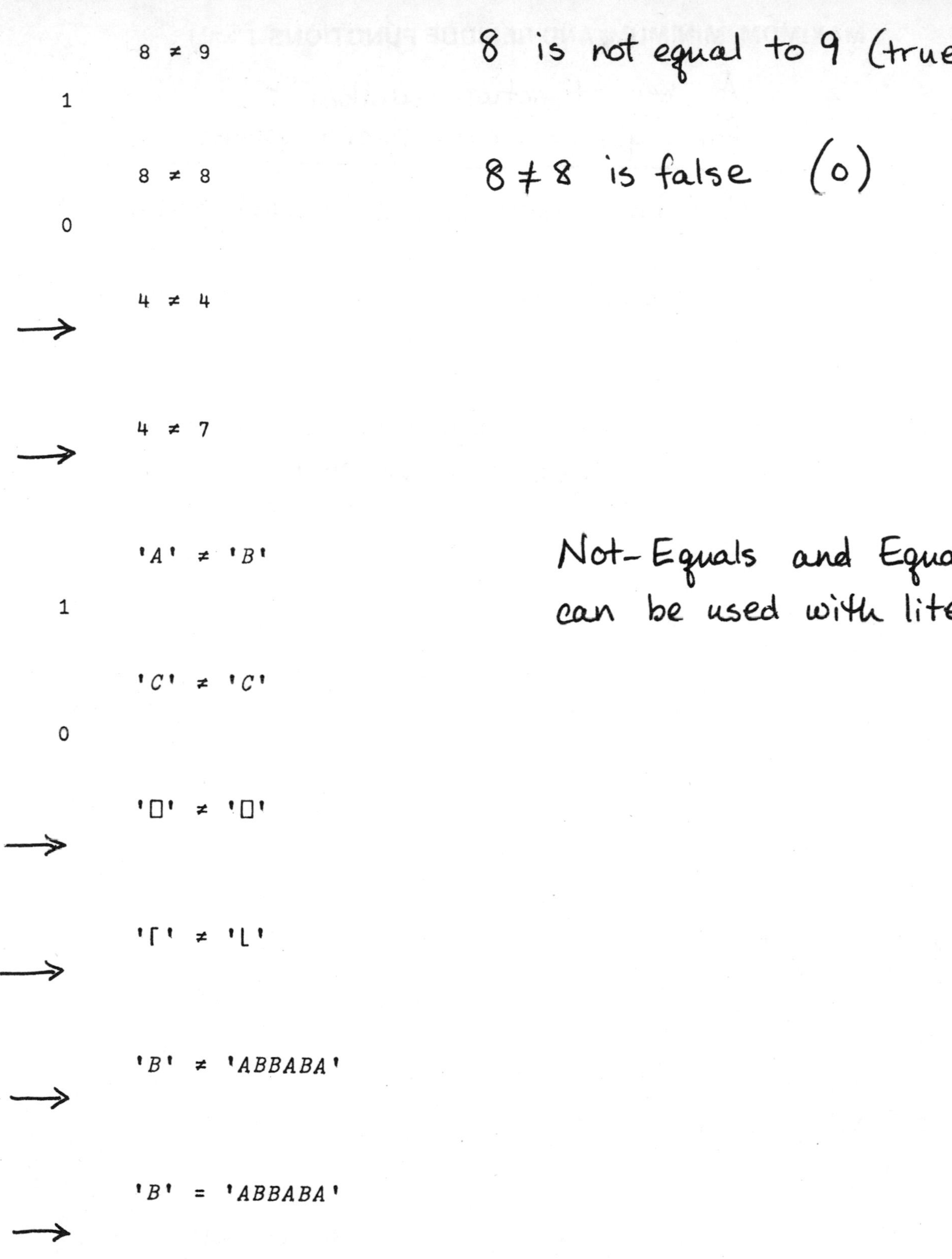

```
      8 ≠ 9
1
      8 ≠ 8
0
      4 ≠ 4
→
      4 ≠ 7
→
      'A' ≠ 'B'
1
      'C' ≠ 'C'
0
      '⎕' ≠ '⎕'
→
      '⌈' ≠ '⌊'
→
      'B' ≠ 'ABBABA'
→
      'B' = 'ABBABA'
→
```

8 is not equal to 9 (true)

8 ≠ 8 is false (0)

Not-Equals and Equals can be used with literals too.

A new function symbol ⌈
for you to experiment with:

```
      8 ⌈ 5
8
```

Use two numbers, one on each side.

```
      5 ⌈ 8
8
```

Try them on opposite sides (commuted)

```
      6 7 8 9 ⌈ 8
8 8 8 9
```

Try several experiments at once (using a vector)

```
      10 ⌈ 8
→

      11 ⌈ 8
11

      12 ⌈ 8
→

      8 ⌈ 12
→

      P ← 2 4 6 4 2
      Q ← 3 2 8 5 1
      P ⌈ Q
3 4 8 5 2
```

⌈ yields the larger of all corresponding elements

⌈ is the <u>Maximum Function</u>

Experiments with ⌊

```
      5 6 7 8 9 10 ⌊ 8
5 6 7 8 8 8

      4 ⌊ 8
→

      8 ⌊ 10 11 3 13
8 8 3 8

      12 ⌊ 8
→

      8 ⌊ 12
→

      P ← 2 4 6 4 2
      Q ← 3 2 8 5 1

      P ⌊ Q
→

      Q ⌊ P
→

      Q ⌈ P
→
```

What does ⌊ do?

What would you call this function?

How does ⌊ relate to ⌈ ?

Challenge:

Here's a challenge!
Figure out how | works.

```
      3 | 8
2

      3 | 0 1 2 3 4 5 6 7
0 1 2 0 1 2 0 1

      3 | 9 10 11
→

      4 | 4 5 6 7 8 9 10 11 12
→

      5 | 5 10 15 20 40 ¯5
0 0 0 0 0 0

      4 | ¯3 ¯2 ¯1 0 1 2 3
1 2 3 0 1 2 3

      5 | ¯6 ¯4 ¯2 0 2 4 6
→

      7 6 5 4 3 2 1 | 14
0 2 4 2 2 0 0
```

REVIEW

In APL, there are two types of *data* which can be represented: literal data, and numerical data. Literal data are represented with enclosing quote marks; numbers are written in the usual way, with decimal points and negative symbols where appropriate.

A variety of *functions* exists in the APL language, perhaps the most fundamental of which are the arithmetic functions and catenation. In addition to these and the relational functions (a family of functions which compare data and result only in 0s or 1s), the maximum, minimum, and residue functions, there are many more to be explored!

All expressions in APL are composed of data and/or functions (usually both together) and can be executed immediately by the computer. This is called the "command execution" mode.

Names may be used—at your discretion—to store data in the computer. The assignment command is used whenever a name is created or whenever data stored in a name are changed. One particularly useful application of this is the use of a *counter* to keep track of a value which is in creased at certain times.

Vectors are linear collections of data and may be either literal or numerical. Through the use of vectors, a single function may be applied to many elements simultaneously. This "parallel processing" is convenient and often useful for experimentation.

Error reports occur whenever you have asked the computer to execute some expression it "doesn't understand." At that point, you may simply retype your expression or enter a new expression. In any event you are not penalized. You may continue as if nothing had happened.

To test your understanding of this first U-Program, try the problems on the next page and check your answers on the computer.

PROBLEMS

```
T ← 3.2  6

S ← 4  ¯2

'T + S'
```
→

```
T + S
```
→

```
T - S
```
→

```
T × S
```
→

```
T ÷ S
```
→

```
T , S
```
→

```
T = S
```
→

```
T < S
```
→

```
T > S
```
→

```
T ≤ S
```
→

```
T ≥ S
```
→

```
T ≠ S
```
→

```
T ⌈ S
```
→

```
T ⌊ S
```
→

```
T | S
```
→

U-Program 2

PROGRAM DEFINITION

Contents

DEFINING A PROGRAM

This is a program to compute the area of a square.

```
      ∇AREA
[1]   'THE AREA IS'
[2]   S × S
[3]   ∇
```

A del ∇ is used to begin program definition and is followed by a <u>name</u>. (This program is named AREA.)

Each expression is entered on successive lines of the program, [1], [2], etc.

A second del ∇ closes program definition.

```
      S ← 6
```

EXECUTING A PROGRAM

```
      AREA
THE AREA IS
36
```

To execute this program, type its name. (AREA)

Then each line is performed by the computer.

(Note that this program required a value for S.)

```
      S ← 7
      AREA
THE AREA IS
49
```

Program AREA can be executed again, perhaps for a different value for S.

```
      S ← 9
      AREA
```

Execute program AREA for S←9

→

```
      S ← 3 4 5 8
      AREA
THE AREA IS
9 16 25 64
```

If S is assigned several values, executing AREA produces results for all values simultaneously.

EDITING A PROGRAM

```
    ∇AREA[1] 'THE AREAS ARE' ∇
```

← Changing line [1]

```
    ∇AREA[⎕]∇
```

← Command to display the (latest) program definition

```
  ∇ AREA
[1]  'THE AREAS ARE'
[2]  S × S
  ∇
```

Note that line [1] has been changed

```
    S ← 1 2 3 4 5
    AREA
THE AREAS ARE
1 4 9 16 25
```

Executing AREA for five values of S

```
    S ← 3 4 5 8
    AREA
```

You Execute AREA now

→

Additional programs may be defined too.

For example, here is another program, named BASEBALL

```
     ∇BASEBALL
[1]  'THIS PROGRAM COMPUTES BATTING AVERAGE.'
[2]  H ÷ AB
[3]  ∇
```

```
     H ← 61
     AB ← 200
     BASEBALL
THIS PROGRAM COMPUTES BATTING AVERAGE.
0.305
```

Note that H and AB must be assigned first, before executing BASEBALL

```
     H ← 63
     AB ← 200
     BASEBALL
```

Execute BASEBALL for these values of H and AB

→

```
      ∇TRIANGLE
[1]   A ← B × H
[2]   A ← .5 × A
[3]   ∇
```

This is another program, named TRIANGLE, which computes the area of a triangle, given its base (B) and height (H). The result will be stored in A.

```
      A
VALUE ERROR
      A
      ^
```

There is no value for A until the program is executed.

```
      B ← 7
      H ← 10
      TRIANGLE
      A
35
```

Executing TRIANGLE does not cause anything to be printed--although the program did do something!

Typing A produces the result.

```
      B ← 6
      H ← 14
      TRIANGLE
      A
→
```

Execute TRIANGLE for the values of B and H assigned.

What is A ?

```
      ∇TRIANGLE
[3]   A
[4]   ∇

      ∇TRIANGLE [⎕]∇
    ∇ TRIANGLE
[1]   A ← B × H
[2]   A ← 0.5 × A
[3]   A
    ∇
```

command to <u>add</u> line(s) to program TRIANGLE

The computer prints [3] for you. You type the expression A. Then, after [4], type a ∇ to end.

The new definition looks like this.

Now line [3] will print the value of A.

```
      B ← 6
      H ← 14
      TRIANGLE
42
```

Executing TRIANGLE now prints the area of a triangle with base 6 and height 14.

```
      B ← 1 2 3 4 5
      H ← 4 8 12 16 20
      TRIANGLE
→
```

Execute TRIANGLE for these 5 bases and 5 heights

Note: When you define a new program, be sure to give it a different name.

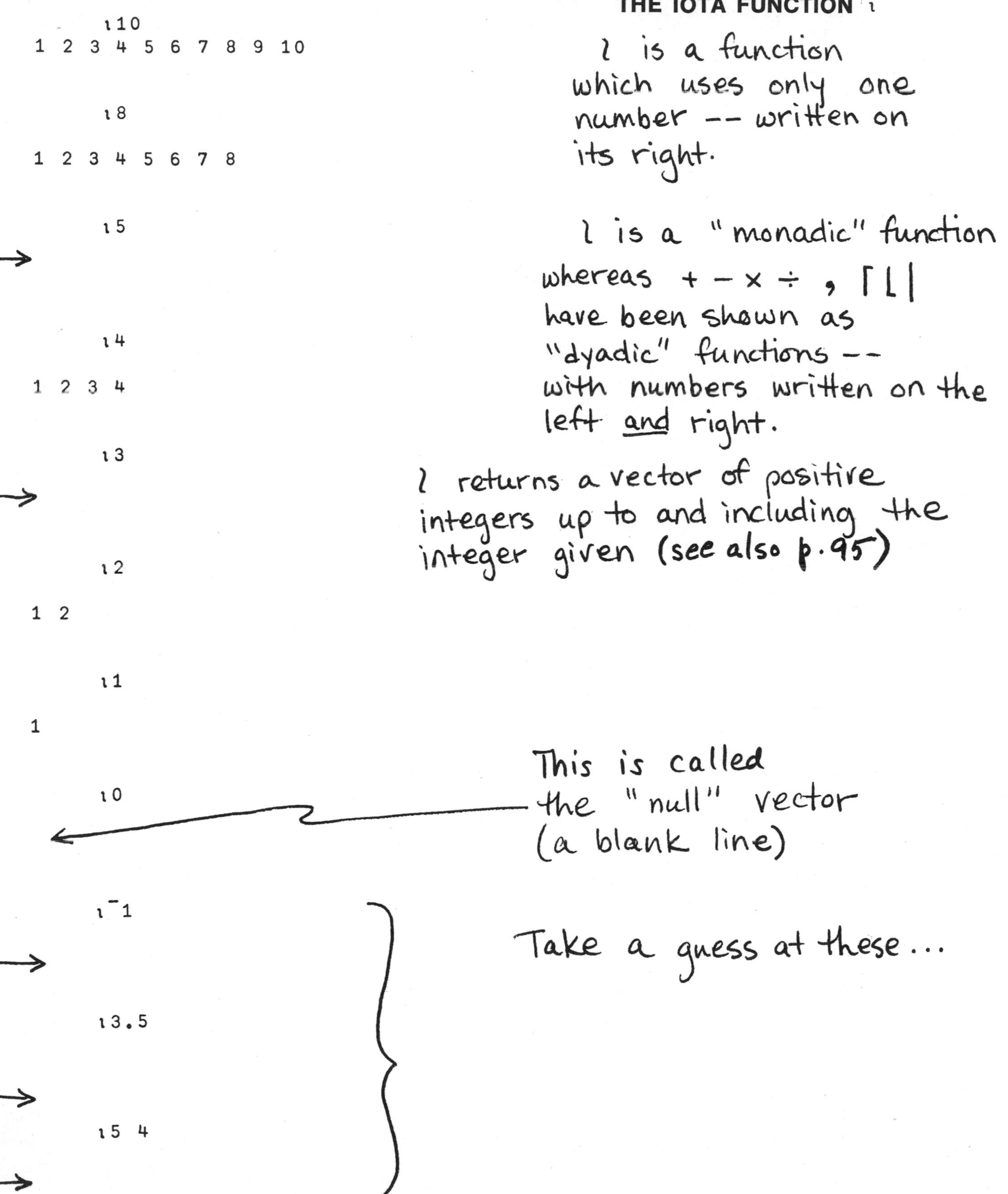

THE IOTA FUNCTION ⍳

⍳ is a function which uses only one number -- written on its right.

⍳ is a "monadic" function whereas + − × ÷ , ⌈ ⌊ | have been shown as "dyadic" functions -- with numbers written on the left and right.

⍳ returns a vector of positive integers up to and including the integer given (see also p.95)

```
      ⍳10
1 2 3 4 5 6 7 8 9 10

      ⍳8
1 2 3 4 5 6 7 8

      ⍳5
→

      ⍳4
1 2 3 4

      ⍳3
→

      ⍳2
1 2

      ⍳1
1

      ⍳0
```

This is called the "null" vector (a blank line)

```
      ⍳¯1
→

      ⍳3.5
→

      ⍳5 4
→
```

Take a guess at these ...

INDEXING [ ]

```
      V ← 2 3 5 7
```

V is a vector of four elements

```
      V[1]
2
```

The first element in V

```
      V[2]
3
```

The second element in V

```
      V[3]
→
```

The third element in V

```
      V[4]
7
```

The fourth element in V

```
      V[5]
→
```

?

```
      ρV
4
```

ρ counts the number of elements

```
      W ← 5 9 2 0 7 1
```

W is assigned some numbers

```
      W[1]
5

      W[2]
→
```

The 2nd element in W

```
      W[3]
→
```

The 3rd element in W

```
      W[2 3]
9 2
```

The 2nd and 3rd elements (an index can be a vector)

```
      W[2 + 3]
→
```

An index can be the result of an expression

```
      W[2] + W[3]
→
```

Add the 2nd and 3rd elements

```
      W[4]
0

      W[5.5]
→
```

The index must be an integer!

```
      W[6]
→

      W[7]
INDEX ERROR
      W[7]
      ^
```

An index cannot be > the total number of elements in the vector.

ρ ("rho") is another monadic function.
It computes the "size" of whatever is written on its right.

```
      X ← ¯7 ¯6 ¯5 ¯4 ¯3 ¯2 ¯1
      ρX
7
```

There are 7 elements in vector X.

```
      Y ← 6 6 6 6 6 6 6 6
      ρY
→
```

How many elements in Y?

```
      ALPHABET ← 'ABCDEFGHIJKLMNOPQRSTUVWXYZ'
      ρALPHABET
26
```

26 letters in ALPHABET

```
      ρ'ABCD'
→

      ρ'A C E'
5
```

ρ Counts spaces too.

```
      SHAKESPEARE ← 'A MIDSUMMER NIGHTS DREAM'
      ρSHAKESPEARE
→
```

Count the literals

```
      TITLE←'A MIDSUMMER NIGHT''S DREAM'
      TITLE
A MIDSUMMER NIGHT'S DREAM
      ρTITLE
25
```

```
      L ← 'TRIAL'

      ρL
5

      L[4]
A

      L[1]
→

      L[5 3 4 2]
LIAR

      L[2 4 1] , ' ' , L[1 4 3 5] , 'S'
→

      L[5] ← 'D'

      L
TRIAD

      L[2 4 5] ← 'WST'

      L
→

      ρL
→
```

The fourth element of L is 'A'

The first element of L is ?

A vector index

Chain these together

Reassign the 5th element of L with 'D'

Now L is

What is L after these reassignments?

How many elements in L ?

```
    V ← 2 3 5 7
```

V is a vector

```
    +/V
17
```

+/ adds up the elements of a vector

```
    2 + 3 + 5 + 7
17
```

It is equivalent to placing + signs between the elements and evaluating the result.

```
    W ← 5 9 2 0 7 1
```

```
    +/W
24
```

+/W adds up the elements in W

```
    5 + 9 + 2 + 0 + 7 + 1
→
```

```
    +/⍳10
55
```

The sum of the integers from 1 to 10

```
    +/⍳9
→
```

Add up the integers from 1 to 9

A MONADIC PROGRAM

DEFINING A PROGRAM TO FIND AVERAGES:

```
      Y ← 4 8 9                ———— Some numbers named Y
      SUM ← +/Y                ———— The sum of the elements in Y
      N ← ρY                   ———— The number of elements in Y
      SUM ÷ N                  ———— The average of the elements in Y
→
```

```
      ∇AVERAGE X
[1]   SUM ← +/X
[2]   N ← ρX
[3]   SUM ÷ N
[4]   ∇
```

A program to find the average of any vector of numbers (X).

Note that the name of the program is AVERAGE and that X stands for the numbers the program will use. To execute this program some numbers must appear to the right of AVERAGE. AVERAGE is, therefore, a "monadic" program.

```
      AVERAGE 4 8 9
7
```

These numbers are the values.

7 is the result.

```
      SUM
→
```

SUM is the sum of the elements in X (from line [1])

```
      N
→
```

N is the number of elements in X (from line [2])

```
      AVERAGE
SYNTAX ERROR
      AVERAGE
      ^
```

AVERAGE requires numbers for X

```
      V ← 2 3 5 7
      AVERAGE V
4.25
```

For values assigned to V, the program prints the AVERAGE of the numbers in V.

```
      W ← 5 9 2 0 7 1
      AVERAGE W
→
```

AVERAGE the numbers in W

```
      W[4] ← 6
      W
→
```

Change the 4th element of W

```
      AVERAGE W
→
```

now AVERAGE W

)*ERASE* — A SYSTEM COMMAND

```
      )ERASE AVERAGE
```

This is a "system command" which will erase any name.

```
      AVERAGE W
SYNTAX ERROR
      AVERAGE W
      ^
```

Now the program AVERAGE is erased

(and a new AVERAGE program could be defined)

Challenge:

Rewrite program AREA as a "monadic" program.
Rewrite program BASEBALL as a "dyadic" program.

REVIEW

The mode of APL in which *programs* are defined is called "program definition" mode (or "function definition" mode). Here expressions may be entered—one line at a time—for execution later by the computer. The sequence of expressions is given a name so that when execution is desired, you need only use that name.

Program definition begins and ends with a del ∇ symbol. (In fact, dels should always be paired, since they act to switch back and forth from command execution mode to program definition mode.) Each expression entered is preceded by a line number, and programs—once defined—may be *edited* by referring to line numbers. For example, lines may be replaced, or new lines may be added. Only the latest version of an edited program is stored by the computer.

Several important points about programs are:

—More than one program may be defined at a given time, but each must have a different name.

—Programs may use values from (global) names assigned either outside or inside a program.

—Results of executed programs may or may not be displayed, depending on their definition.

Some additional primitive functions, helpful in defining programs, are: iota ⍳ , rho ⍴, indexing [ ], and sum-reduction +/. Iota generates index integers beginning with 1 (unless directed otherwise); rho computes the size of numerical or literal data (e.g., the number of elements in a vector); indexing is used to select individual elements of data (numerical or literal); and sum-reduction adds up numbers. Iota and rho are examples of "monadic" functions.

All monadic functions in APL appear with data only on the right hand side. They differ from "dyadic" functions, such as + − × ÷, which are used with data on both sides. From syntax alone, then, you can distinguish between monadic and dyadic functions.

Programs may be defined to be monadic or dyadic or nyladic (the latter meaning no input data).

To test your understanding of U-Program 2, execute (by hand) the program on the next page. Check your results against the computer's.

```
      S ← 9

      V ← 2 3 5 7 11 13

      L ← 'AEHNRSTW '

      ∇REVIEW

[1] L[7 3 2 9 1 4 6 8 2 5 6 9 1 5 2]

[2]  ρL

[3]  ρV

[4]  ⍳S

[5]  V[4] - V[1]

[6]  V[3] + ρV

[7]  +/V[5-2 3]

[8]  +/V

[9]  +/⍳S

[10] V[ρV]

[11] V[⍳ρV]

[12] +/V[⍳ρV]

[13] +/V[ρV]-S

[14] +/⍳V[3]+ρV

      ∇

      REVIEW

→
```

U-Program 3

EVALUATING EXPRESSIONS

Contents

```
     5 + 4 × 2
13

     5 + (4 × 2)
13

     (5 + 4) × 2
18

     (10 × 3) + 4
34

     10 × (3 + 4)
70

     10 × 3 + 4
70

     (6 × 4) + 5
→

     6 × (4 + 5)
→

     6 × 4 + 5
→

     6 + 4 × 5
→

     6 + (4 × 5)
→
```

When two (or more) functions occur in one expression, the rules for evaluation are:

RULE 1:

The function inside parentheses is done first.

RULE 2: Inside the parentheses (or when there are none)

the <u>rightmost</u> function is done first.

Do 6 × 4 first

Do 4 + 5 first

Do 4 + 5 first

Do 4 × 5 first

6 plus (4 times 5)

```
      (2 × 3) + (4 × 5)
26

      (2 × 3) + 4 × 5
26

      2 × 3 + 4 × 5
46
```

first ——— 4×5
then —— 3 + 20
then 2 × 23

```
      1 + 10 × 9 - 2
71

      1 + (10 × (9 - 2))
71
```

These are equivalent expressions

```
      (2 × 3 + 5 × 4) = (2 × (3 + (5 × 4)))
→
```

Are these two expressions equal?

Challenge:

```
      Z1 ← 3 × 8 ⌊ 5 + 4 ÷¯2
      Z2 ← 3 × (8 ⌊ (5 + (4 ÷¯2)))

      Z1 = Z2
1

      Z1
→
```

```
⍳6 + 5 | 4 × ¯3 ⌈ 2
```

A Long expression

```
T ← ¯3 ⌈ 2
T
```

Evaluation by pieces:

→

```
S ← 4 × T
S
```

→

```
R ← 5 | S
R
```

→

```
Q ← 6 + R
Q
```

→

```
P ← ⍳Q
P
```

→

Evaluating expressions in APL is different from the way it is done in algebra (× and ÷ first, then + and −).

One reason for this is that there are so many functions in APL (about 60 in all!) that it would be hard to remember which to do first.

This is how sum-reduction is actually evaluated:

```
      W ← 5 9 2 6 7 1
      +/W
30

      5 + 9 + 2 + 6 + 7 + 1
→

      5 + (9 + (2 + (6 + (7 + 1))))
→

      SUM ← 1
      SUM
→

      SUM ← 7 + SUM
      SUM
→

      SUM ← 6 + SUM
      SUM
→

      SUM ← 2 + SUM
      SUM
→

      SUM ← 9 + SUM
      SUM
→

      SUM ← 5 + SUM
      SUM
→
```

Some other dyadic functions may be used with the reduction symbol /.

Times-reduction

```
      W ← 5 9 2 6 7 1
      ×/W
3780
      5 × 9 × 2 × 6 × 7 × 1
```

→

×/ is evaluated like +/ (only with × in place of +)

Maximum-reduction

⌈/ is evaluated similarly

```
      ⌈/W
9
      5 ⌈ 9 ⌈ 2 ⌈ 6 ⌈ 7 ⌈ 1
9
      MAX ← 7 ⌈ 1
      MAX
```

→

```
      MAX ← 6 ⌈ MAX
      MAX
```

→

```
      MAX ← 2 ⌈ MAX
      MAX
```

→

```
      MAX ← 9 ⌈ MAX
      MAX
```

→

```
      MAX ← 5 ⌈ MAX
      MAX
```

→

(This is the largest value in the vector)

Minimum-reduction

```
W ← 5 9 2 6 7 1
⌊/W
```
→

⌊/

also

evaluates from

"right to left"

```
MIN ← 7 ⌊ 1
MIN ← 6 ⌊ MIN
MIN ← 2 ⌊ MIN
MIN ← 9 ⌊ MIN
MIN ← 5 ⌊ MIN
MIN
```
→

(This is the <u>smallest</u> value in the vector)

Minus-reduction

```
-/W
¯2
```

Note that the result here is <u>not</u> the same as the algebraic sum of the numbers.

```
5 - 9 - 2 - 6 - 7 - 1
¯2
```

The rightmost operation is done first,

```
DIFF ← 7 - 1
DIFF
```
→

then the next rightmost,

```
DIFF ← 6 - DIFF
DIFF
```
→

then the next rightmost,

```
DIFF ← 2 - DIFF
DIFF
```
→

⋮

and so on

⋮

```
DIFF ← 9 - DIFF
DIFF
```
→

until the last operation is completed.

```
DIFF ← 5 - DIFF
DIFF
```
→

```
      -/⍳6
→
      R ← 5 - 6
      R ← 4 - R
      R ← 3 - R
      R ← 2 - R
      R ← 1 - R
      R
¯3
```

minus-reduction of 1 2 3 4 5 6

step by step

__Challenge:__

```
      S ← ⍳6
      (+/S[1 3 5]) - +/S[2 4 6]
→

      +/⍳6
→

      -/⍳6
→

      ×/⍳6
→

      ÷/⍳6
→

      ⌈/⍳6
→

      ⌊/⍳6
→

      |/⍳6
→
```

Reduction is generalized for use with dyadic functions + − × ÷ ⌈ ⌊ and | etc.

Check yourself on the rules for evaluating expressions

```
      ⍳4
→
      2 × ⍳4
→
      ⍳4 × 2
→
      (⍳4) × 2
→
      3 + 2 × ⍳4
→
      +/3 + 2 × ⍳4
32

      CENTIGRADE ← 20 + 10 × ¯1 + ⍳4
      CENTIGRADE
→

     FAHRENHEIT ← 32 + 9 × CENTIGRADE ÷ 5
     FAHRENHEIT
→
```

REVIEW

APL has simple rules for evaluating expressions—even those containing many different functions. Basically, the rule is to evaluate the function on the far *right*—subject to parentheses, which dominate in the normal way—and repeat until the entire expression is done. There is no hierarchy of functions in APL (as there is in conventional algebra).

Another way of viewing the APL rule for evaluating expressions is the following: Every function—dyadic or monadic—uses the entire expression on its right. (This amounts to evaluating the rightmost function first.)

Reduction operation is generalized to apply to many dyadic functions, including + - × ÷ ⌈ ⌊ and | . The / notation is always preceded by a dyadic function which is (effectively) inserted between elements of the data following, and then the resulting expression is evaluated.

Test your understanding of these APL rules by evaluating the expressions on the next page.

PROBLEMS

```
R ← 5 5 10 4 5 20

E ← 3

V ← 2 3 5 7 11 13

I ← 2

E ← 4

W ← 5 9 2 6 7 1


      ιE
→

      I × ιE
→

      ιE × I
→

      (ιE) × I
→

      E + I × ιE
→

      +/E + I × ιE
→

      E + I × E - I
→

      (E + I) × E - I
→

      (E + I) × (E - I)
→

      +/V × W
→

      -/R < W
→

      (⌈/W) - ⌊/W
→

→     (+/W) ÷ ρW

      R ⌊ E ⌊ V ⌊ I ⌊ E ⌊ W
→

      ⌊/R , E , V , I , E , W
→
```

U-Program 4

BRANCHING

Contents

```
      L ← 1 1 0 0

      K ← 1 0 1 0

      L ∧ K
1 0 0 0

      1 ∧ 1
→
      1 ∧ 0
→
      0 ∧ 1
→
      0 ∧ 0
→
```

The AND function ∧

The result is 1 for both 1 <u>and</u> 1; 0 otherwise.

```
      L ∨ K
1 1 1 0

      1 ∨ 1
→
      1 ∨ 0
→
      0 ∨ 1
→
      0 ∨ 0
→
```

The OR function ∨

The result is 1 if one <u>or</u> the other (or both) is 1; 0 otherwise.

```
      ~L
0 0 1 1

      ~1
→
      ~0
→
```

The NOT function ~

The result is the logical opposite.

The LOGICAL functions (AND, OR, NOT) only operate on logical data (0s and 1s).

```
      ~L ∨ K
0 0 0 1
```

"NOT" (L "OR" K)

```
      ~L ∧ K
```

"NOT" (L "AND" K)

→

```
      (~L) ∧ ~K
```

("NOT" L) "AND" ("NOT" K)

→

Challenge:

```
      +/~(L ∧ ~K) ∧ L ∨ ~L = K
```

→

```
      L
1 1 0 0
      K
1 0 1 0
      ∧/L
0
      ∧/K
→
      ∧/L=L
1
      ∨/L
1
      ∨/K
→
      ∨/L≠L
0
```

And-reduction

∧/1 1 0 0 is equivalent to 1∧1∧0∧0

∧/ yields 1 if and only if all 1s follow; 0 otherwise.

∨/ yields 1 if any 1 follows.

Or-reduction

∨/ yields 0 if all 0s follow.

→ $\wedge/L\vee K$ Does $L \vee K$ result in all 1s?

→ $\vee/L\wedge K$ Does $L \wedge K$ result in any 1s?

```
      Q ← K , L
      Q
1 0 1 0 1 1 0 0
```

Values of K and L are chained together and named Q

```
      P ← 2 3 5 7 11 13 17 19
      P
2 3 5 7 11 13 17 19
```

```
      Q × P
```

→

The COMPRESSION function /

```
      Q / P
2 5 11 13
```

This expression may be read as: "Q compress P". Only those elements in P which have corresponding 1s in Q appear in the result

```
      (~Q) / P
3 7 17 19
```

Here the result is elements in P where 1s appear on the left:

	↓		↓			↓	↓
0	1	0	1	0	0	1	1
2	3	5	7	11	13	17	19

Note: The COMPRESSION function requires a logical vector of 0s and 1s on the left -- one for each element on the right.

```
      L
1 1 0 0

      K
1 0 1 0

      L / 6 2 8 4
6 2

      K / 6 2 8 4
→

      L / 'HITS'
HI

      K / 'FLIP'
→

      1 0 0 0 0 1 0 1 0 1 1 0 1 0 0 / 'STOP THE RECORD'
→
```

COMPRESSION works by:
- keeping values where there are 1s
- omitting values where there are 0s

1	1	0	0
6	2	8	4
(keep)	(keep)	(omit)	(omit)

Keep the values where there are 1s in K

COMPRESSION works similarly with literals

```
      1 1 / 3 5
3 5
```

Keep the 3 and the 5

```
      1 0 / 3 5
```

→ Keep the 3; omit the 5

```
      0 1 / 3 5
```

→ Omit the 3; keep the 5

```
      0 0 / 3 5
```

→ Omit the 3 and the 5

```
      1 / 6
6

      0 / 6
```

COMPRESSION of a single element either returns that element -- as in 1/6 or returns the <u>null vector</u> -- as in 0/6

This fact is used in branching.

Program POW computes and prints four powers of N by repeated multiplication

```
      ∇POW
[1]   Z ← 1
[2]   Z ← Z × N   ⎤
[3]   Z           ⎦
[4]   Z ← Z × N   ⎤
[5]   Z           ⎦
[6]   Z ← Z × N   ⎤
[7]   Z           ⎦
[8]   Z ← Z × N   ⎤
[9]   Z ∇         ⎦
```

Note: You may end program definition with a ∇ on the end of the last line.

```
      N ← 3
      POW
3     ——— caused by line [3]
9     ———    "   "   "  [5]
27    ———    "   "   "  [7]
81    ———    "   "   "  [9]
```

```
      N ← 4
      POW
```

Execute POW for N←4

→

```
      ∇POWOW
[1]   Z ← 1
[2]   Z ← Z × N
[3]   Z
[4]   →2 ∇

      N ← 4

      POWOW
4
16
64
256
1024
4096
16384
65536
262144
1048576
4194304
16777216
67108864
268435456
1073741824
4294967296
  •
  •
  •
```

Program POWOW accomplishes what program POW does (and more) by iteration ; that is, it repeats certain statements by using an unconditional branch command.

Line [4] →2 can be read as: "go to line [2]" and causes the program to repeat lines [2] and [3] (indefinitely) . . . .

This is known as an "endless loop"-- a programmer's nightmare!

Push ATTN key (on top right of keyboard) to stop the computer printing

POWOW should be edited so that it will stop after a certain number of repititions.

```
      ∇POWOW [1.5] I ← 0
[1.6] [3.5]   I ← I + 1
[3.6] [4]   →(I < 9)/3∇
```

This command inserts a new line between lines [1] and [2] (You are then given the opportunity on [1.6] to insert more lines.)

Line [1.6] may be overridden to insert a new line between lines [3] and [4].

(Again, [3.6] invites you to insert more lines.)

Overriding with a new line [4] replaces what was on line [4].

```
      ∇POWOW[⎕]∇

    ∇ POWOW
[1]   Z ← 1
[2]   I ← 0
[3]   Z ← Z × N
[4]   Z
[5]   I ← I + 1
[6]   →(I < 9)/3
    ∇
```

Now, displaying the whole program POWOW includes the new lines.

Also, note that the lines have been automatically renumbered.

```
      ∇POWOW[⎕]∇

    ∇ POWOW
[1]   Z ← 1
[2]   I ← 0
[3]   Z ← Z × N
[4]   Z
[5]   I ← I + 1
[6]   →(I < 9)/3
    ∇

      N ← 4
      POWOW
4
16
64
256
1024
4096
16384
65536
262144
```

I is initialized as 0.

I is incremented by 1 (each iteration.)

I is a "counter" used to count how many times lines [3] and [4] are executed.

Line [6] is a conditional branch command

it can be read as:
"branch to line [3] if I is less than 9 -- otherwise, go to the next line"

The general format is
→(condition)/ line number

(Note that branching works this way because of the compression function.)

Now, the program stops after printing 9 powers of N.

```
∇POWOW[6] →(I < X) / 3∇
```

Editing POWOW again so that it will stop after a certain number of iterations.

Line [6] is changed.

```
N ← 8

X ← 12
```

X is a name used by the program and therefore must be assigned a value.

```
POWOW
8
64
512
4096
32768
262144
2097152
16777216
134217728
1073741824
8589934592
6.871947674E10
```

Here X is 12 (iterations)

Note that large numbers -- here, larger than 10 billion -- displayed in E notation (similar to "scientific notation") where E may be read as "...times ten to the..." The same holds for very small numbers -- like one billionth is 1E¯9.

```
N ← 5

X ← 4

POWOW
```

X can be easily changed (as can N)

You execute it.

→

Program POWOW may be changed so that the values for N and X can be entered at the same time as the program name.

```
      ∇POWOW[0] N POWOW X ∇
```

This editing command is used to change line [0] (the "header" of the program)

```
      ∇POWOW [0] N POWER X ∇
```

or, even the name of the program can be changed.

```
      ∇POWER[⎕]∇
    ∇ N POWER X
[1]   Z ← 1
[2]   I ← 0
[3]   Z ← Z × N
[4]   Z
[5]   I ← I + 1
[6]   →(I < X)/3
    ∇
```

Now POWER is a new "dyadic" program

```
      5 POWER 4
5
25
125
625
```

It uses two values:
one on the left (for N)
one on the right (for X)

Notice that each value for Z is printed (due to line [4]).

```
      ∇POWER[4]
[4]
[5]   ∇
```

This is the procedure for deleting a line: cause the computer to type the line number and then press ATTN, followed immediately by RETURN. That line will be deleted; and all lines affected in the program will be renumbered after the final del ∇.

```
      5 POWER 4
```

If line [4] is deleted, program POWER will not print anything...

```
      Z
625
```

although the final result can be obtained by typing Z.

If the header of a program assigns a value, it has an "explicit result".

```
∇POWER[0] Z ← N POWER X ∇
```

POWER is changed to have an explicit result (Z).

```
      3 POWER 2
9
```

When POWER is executed, now whatever value Z has at the end of the program is printed as the result.

Only the final value of Z is printed

The program itself has this result. The importance of this is that the program can now be used in expressions.

(see page 68)

```
      2 POWER 3
→
```

Execute POWER for an N of 2 and an X of 3

```
      ∇POWER[⎕]∇
    ∇ Z ← N POWER X
[1]   Z ← 1
[2]   I ← 0
[3]   Z ← Z × N
[4]   I ← I + 1
[5]   →(I < X)/3
    ∇
```

The display of POWER

Z is <u>local</u> to the program (as are N and X); they are only placeholders for values the program will use when executed. They do not keep their values outside of the program. (See also p. 81)

```
      3 POWER 2
9
```

When POWER is executed, the result is only temporarily assigned to Z.

```
      Z
625
```

As soon as the program terminates, Z returns to its previously assigned value (see p. 61)

```
      N
5
```

Similarly for N and X (see p. 59)

```
      X
4
```

```
    TΔPOWER ← ⍳5
    5 POWER 4
POWER[1]  1
POWER[2]  0
POWER[3]  5
POWER[4]  1
POWER[5]  3
POWER[3]  25
POWER[4]  2
POWER[5]  3
POWER[3]  125
POWER[4]  3
POWER[5]  3
POWER[3]  625
POWER[4]  4
POWER[5]
625
```

Command to "trace" lines 1 thru 5 of program POWER

When the program is traced, all results of execution-- for each line indicated-- are printed out.

POWER[5] — (a null vector)

625 — the final result (Z)

```
    TΔPOWER ← 0
    5 POWER 4
625
```

TΔPOWER ← 0 — Removing the trace

Normal execution

```
    5 * 4
625
```

Program POWER simulates the behavior of the primitive function * for positive integers on the right.

THE POWER FUNCTION *

```
      3 * 2
9
```

3 "to the power" 2
(3 squared)

```
      4 * 2
16
```

4 "to the power" 2
(4 squared)

```
      6 * 2
```

6 "to the power" 2

→

```
      5 7 9 * 2
25 49 81
```

Several numbers to the power 2

```
      5 * ι5
5 25 125 625 3125
```

5 to several powers

```
      7 8 9 10 * 1 2 3 4
```

Several numbers to several different powers

→

```
      3 * 3
27
```

3 "to the power" 3
(3 cubed)

```
      3 × 3 × 3
```

→

```
      3 * 4
```

3 "to the power" 4

→

```
      3 × 3 × 3 × 3
```

→

```
      3 * 5
243
```

3 to the 5th power

```
      25 16 49 * .5
5 4 7
```
Square roots (numbers to the $\frac{1}{2}$ power)

```
      9 * .5
→
```

```
      ¯16 * .5
→
```

```
      ¯8 * 1 ÷ 3
→
```
Cube root

```
      32 * 1 ÷ 5
2
```
Fifth root

```
      412 * 0.35
8.22647961
```
Fractional powers are permitted

```
      2 * ¯1
→
```
Negative powers (2^{-1} or $\frac{1}{2^1}$)

```
      16 * ¯.5
0.25
```

```
      0 * 0
→
```
An APL curiosity (Take a guess)

Three different absolute value programs ("absolute value" is the positive value of a number):

① ABSOLUTEVALUE using *

```
    ∇ABSOLUTEVALUE
[1] (X * 2) * .5∇

    X ← 8 ¯8
    ABSOLUTEVALUE
8 8
```

② ABsolute value using branching

```
    ∇AB X
[1] →(X < 0) / 4  ——— if X is a negative number, go to 4 and
[2] X             ——— otherwise, print X and then
[3] →0            ——— stop
[4] -X ∇          ——— print the negative of X

    AB 8
→

    AB ¯8
→
```

Note →0 (or any other line number not in the program) causes it to stop immediately.

③ ABSolute value using explicit result.

```
    ∇Z ← ABS X
[1] Z ← X           ——— assume X is a positive number and make that number the result (Z)
[2] →(X > 0) / 0    ——— if X is positive, stop
[3] Z ← -X ∇        ——— otherwise, the result (Z) is changed to the negative of X

    ABS ¯11
11

    ABS 11
→
```

```
      |¯8
8
      |8.88
8.88
      |¯3 × ¯3
→
      |3 × ¯3
→
      |5 × ¯8
40
      ABS 5 × ¯8
40
      T ← ABS ¯340 ÷17
      T
20
      T ← AB ¯340 ÷17
20
SYNTAX ERROR
      T←AB ¯340÷17
       ∧
```

| returns a positive number

The defined function ABS performs identically to | and can be used in expressions . . .

whereas program AB cannot (because it has no explicit result)

Challenge: Defined program RES models the residue function (see p. 16)
(see also p.200 for the formal definition of |.)

```
     ∇R ← A RES B
[1]  →((A = 0) ∧ B < 0) / 0
[2]  R ← B
[3]  →(A = 0) / 0
[4]  R ← R - |A
[5]  →(R ≥ 0) / 4
[6]  R ← R + |A
[7]  →(R < 0) / 6 ∇
```

[1] if A is 0 and B is negative, stop (residue is not defined)

[3] if A is 0, branch to 0 (stop); the result is B

[4]–[5] if R is ≥0, subtract absolute values of A repeatedly

[6]–[7] if R is negative, add absolute values of A repeatedly until R is nonnegative.

```
     5 RES 13
```

→ You try it for 5 and 13

Tracing RES

```
     T∆RES ← ⍳7

     5 RES 13
RES[1]
RES[2]  13
RES[3]
RES[4]  8
RES[5]  4
RES[4]  3
RES[5]  4
RES[4]  ¯2
RES[5]
RES[6]  3
RES[7]
3
```

Removing the trace

```
     T∆RES ← 0
```

```
      5 RES 13
→
      5 | 13
→
```

These are equivalent

```
      1 RES 3.14
0.14
```

This yields the fractional part

```
      3.14 - 1 RES 3.14
→
```

RES can be used in an expression . . .

```
      3.14 - 1 | 3.14
3
```

. . . just like the | function.

Challenge:

```
      ∇D ← FLOOR  N
[1]   D ← N - 1|N
      ∇
      FLOOR  3.14
→
```

```
      ∇S ← CEILING  N
[1]   S ← N + 1|-N
      ∇
      CEILING  3.14
→
```

The FLOOR Function ⌊

```
      ⌊3.14
3

      ⌊6.2 6.4 6.6 6.8 7.0 7.2
6 6 6 6 7 7

      ⌊8.0 8.3 8.6 8.9 9.2 9.5
→
```

Floor yields the nearest integer down the number line. (≤)

The CEILING Function ⌈

```
      ⌈3.14
4

      ⌈6.2 6.4 6.6 6.8 7.0 7.2
7 7 7 7 7 8

      ⌈8.0 8.3 8.6 8.9 9.2 9.5
→
```

Ceiling yields the nearest integer up the number line. (≥)

```
      SHERLOCK ← 'SCOTLAND YARD'
      H ← 7 4 11 21 5 12
      SHERLOCK[⌈35 × H ÷+/H]
LONDON
```

An example of using ⌈ in indexing (it assures you that the indices are integers)

A program to ROUND off numbers to the nearest integer

```
     ∇Q ← ROUND N
[1]  Q ← ⌊N + 0.5 ∇
```

```
     ROUND 3.14
```

```
     ROUND 3.6
```

```
     ROUND ¯2.55
```

```
     ROUND ¯2.0904
```

Challenge:

⎕← displays the result of the expression to its right.

```
     ⎕ ← X ← 10 ÷ 6
1.666666667

     (10 * ¯3) × ⌊0.5 + X × 10 * 3
1.667

     (10 * ¯4) × ⌊0.5 + X × 10 * 4
```

→

REVIEW

Branching is an important programming technique. It permits you to indicate the sequence of commands to be executed in a program. Both unconditional and conditional branching can be expressed. A popular form of conditional branch commands is → (condition) / (line #) although any expression which evaluates to an integer or null may follow the branch symbol →.

The logical functions ∧ (AND), ∨ (OR), ~ (NOT), and the compression function / are often used within branch commands. Also, the power function ⋆ , absolute value | (monadic), residue | (dyadic), ceiling ⌈ , and floor ⌊ are useful mathematical tools available on the keyboard. It should be noted that some APL functions serve double duty—that is, they can be used monadically or dyadically.

Additional program editing procedures include inserting new lines between existing lines, deleting lines, and changing the header of a program.

Programs with "explicit results" can be used within expressions just as if they were primitive functions on the keyboard. You may define such programs with local names—names which have values only while the program is being executed. The complete execution of a program (or any specified lines) may be *traced* automatically by the computer.

Test your understanding of branching and related functions with the exercises on the following page.

PROBLEMS

```
0 0 0 0 1 1 0 0 0 0 0 1 1 1 1 0 0 0 0 0 0/'BEFORE YOU VIEW MORE,'
→

(4 = 4) ∧ 5 = 5
→

(3 ≥ 4) ∨ 5 ≠ 5
→

LOGICAL ← 0 1 1 0 0 1

(~ ∧/LOGICAL) = ∨/~LOGICAL
→

2 | +/LOGICAL
→

2 * +/LOGICAL
→

| +/LOGICAL
→

| -/LOGICAL
→

⎕ ← S ← 3
→
⎕ ← T ← (S ≠ ⍳S + 1) / ⍳S + 1
→

T * S
→

S * T
→

(S * 2 ) ⌈ 2 * S
→

((S + 1) * 2) = (S  * 2) + (2 × S) + 1
→

(S × ×/S - T) * .5
→
```

```
⎕ ← P ← 2
```

→

```
⎕ ← X ← 20 ÷ 3
```

→

```
(10 * -P) × ⌊.5 + X × 10 * P
```

→

Embody the above expression in a program (with an explicit result) which will round-off a number X to P places.

→

Examine the program below

```
      ∇Z ← L MAX R
[1]    → (L > R) /4
[2]    Z ← R
[3]    → 0
[4]    Z ← L
    ∇
```

and then write a similar program (with branching) to find the MINimum of two numbers L and R.

→

Then,

```
TΔMIN ← ⍳4
R ← 1.667 MIN 2
```

→

```
TΔMIN ← 0
S MIN R MAX T [S]
```

→

U-Program 5

APPLYING FUNCTIONS

Contents

```
      ?2
2
      ?2
1
      ?2
1
      ?2
→
      ?3 3 3 3 3 3 3 3
1 1 2 3 1 2 1 3
      ?6 6 6 6 6
6 4 5 4 3
      ?52
→
      (?52) = ?52
0
      N ← ?52
      (1 ≤ N) ∧ (N ≤ 52) ∧ 0 = 1 | N
1
      N
29
```

?2 returns a 1 or 2 (randomly) -- it is hard to predict which.

Random integers from 1 to 3

A random number from 1 to 52 (picked out of ⍳52)

You may not get the same number if you execute ?52 twice

If N is some integer between 1 and 52, then N is ≥ 1 and N is ≤ 52 and N is a whole number (remainder after dividing by 1 is 0)

see?

```
      ? 6 6
2 5

      ?6 6
→

      ∇Z ← ROLL
[1]   Z ← +/ ?6 6 ∇

      ROLL
7

      ROLL
11

      ROLL
6

      ROLL
→

      ROLL
→
```

Simulating the roll of two dice

Two random numbers, each between 1 and 6

A program to ROLL two "dice" and add them up.

(ROLL is a "nyladic" program with an explicit result Z.)

Lucky!

"Roll" two dice and add the numbers

Again — (it may be a different result)

```
      ALPHABET ← 'ABCDEFGHIJKLMNOPQRSTUVWXYZ'

      ALPHABET[?26]
K
```

Randomly picking a letter from the ALPHABET

```
      ALPHABET[?ρALPHABET]
→
```

A random index (1 to 26)

```
      ALPHABET[?26 26 26 26]
QVAR
```

4 random indices

```
      ALPHABET[?26 26 26 26]
→
```

LOCAL NAMES

```
      ∇ RANDOMWORDS N ; J
[1]   J ← 0
[2]   ALPHABET[?26 26 26 26]
[3]   J ← J + 1
[4]  → (J < N) /2 ∇
```

N is a local name. Additional local names may be listed after semicolons in the program header.

[1] Initially J is 0

[2] 4 random letters are printed

[3] J is incremented by 1

[4] branch to line 2 if J<N otherwise end the program

J is a local name used by the program RANDOMWORDS (in addition to N)

```
      RANDOMWORDS 6
QPXL
KJDG
ROHJ
RSCK
XBVE
CSXY
```

RANDOMWORDS prints N randomly generated 4-letter "words"

J is used to count (inside the program) the random "words"

```
      J
VALUE ERROR
      J
      ^
```

Note that J has no value outside the program

```
      N
29
```

And N is not changed (This is the value of N from page 78)

`4 ∊ 2 4 6 8`	Is 4 a member of 2 4 6 8 ?
`1`	(Yes)
`5 ∊ 2 4 6 8`	Is 5 a member of 2 4 6 8 ?
`0`	(No)
`6 ∊ ⍳5`	Is 6 a member of 1 2 3 4 5 ?
→	
`2 ∊ ⍳5`	Is 2 a member of 1 2 3 4 5 ?
→	
`VOWELS ← 'AEIOU'`	
`'A' ∊ VOWELS`	Is 'A' a member of 'AEIOU' ?
`1`	(Yes)
`'B' ∊ VOWELS`	Is 'B' a vowel ?
→	
`'CAT' ∊ VOWELS`	3 questions: Is 'C' a vowel ? (no) Is 'A' a vowel ? (yes) Is 'T' a vowel ? (no)
`0 1 0`	
`'COMPUTER' ∊ VOWELS`	give 8 answers (0s and 1s)
→	
`∨/ 'COMPUTER' ∊ VOWELS`	There is at least one vowel in 'COMPUTER'
`1`	

```
      ∨/ 'LINGO' ∊ VOWELS
→
```

∨/ 0 1 0 0 1

```
      ∇Z ← VOWELCHECKER WORD
  [1] Z ← ∨/ WORD ∊ VOWELS ∇
```

A program to check if a WORD has a VOWEL

```
      VOWELCHECKER 'CONSONANTS'
→
```

Is there a vowel in 'CONSONANTS'? (yes or no)

```
      VOWELCHECKER 'WHYZZ'
→
```

0 or 1 ?

Programs may be used within other programs. They are called "sub-programs".

```
    ∇ RW
[1]   WORD ← ALPHABET [?26 26 26 26]
[2]   → (0 = VOWELCHECKER WORD) /1
[3]   WORD
[4]   →1
    ∇
```

Program VOWELCHECKER is used within program RW as a sub-program.

It checks WORD (a random 4-letter "word" assigned on line [1]) for a vowel. If it doesn't have a vowel (0= VOWELCHECKER WORD) the program branches back to line [1] to pick another WORD. If it does have a vowel, the next line [3] prints the WORD before going back to line [1] again.

Remember that VOWELCHECKER must have an explicit result in order to be used in an expression.

```
      RW
PVIG
ZWWI
YRVO
OEYV
EBIC
CNAO
SAER
IBDX
FJPE
ARTS
EZOH
OPRM
OPLD
NTAB
NIAG
CJOP
PYUN
PUXR
XGQA
CLIH
TIIB
OMFC
UFEB
LKQI
XUEO
AUNW
PTWI
ETSW
CEKC
ROVW
UQXW
JWUL
FDFI
```

Now, here are some random 4-letter words with vowels

•

•

•

•

•

Uh oh. This program has no way of stopping.

You might edit RW to count the WORDs printed out and to stop when it reaches a certain number (like RANDOMWORDS on page 81)

For now, use the ATTN key to stop it.

THE TAKE FUNCTION ↑

```
      W ← 5 9 2 6 7 1
      2 ↑ W
5 9
      3 ↑ W
5 9 2
      4 ↑ W
→
      5 ↑ W
5 9 2 6 7
      W = 6 ↑ W
→
      7 ↑ W
5 9 2 6 7 1 0
      ¯2 ↑ W
7 1
      ¯3 ↑ W
→
      (2 ↑ W) , ¯4 ↑ W
5 9 2 6 7 1
      ¯5 ↑ W
→
      ¯8 ↑ W
→
```

2 "take" W
(take the first 2 from the front of W)

3 "take" W

4 "take" W

W is compared to 6 "take" W

When taking more than the total number of elements, 0s are used (or spaces, with literal arrays).

Take 2 from the rear of W

Take the last 3 of W

The last 5 of W

(Guess)

```
      W
5 9 2 6 7 1

      2 ↓ W
2 6 7 1

      3 ↓ W
→

      (4 ↓ W) = ¯2 ↑ W
1 1

      (¯2 ↓ W) = 4 ↑ W
1 1 1 1

      ¯4 ↓ W
→

      ¯6 ↓ W
→

      ¯3 ↓ 'APLOMB'
APL

      3 ↑ 'APLOMB'
→
```

2 "drop" W
(drop the first 2 from the front of W)

Drop the first 3 from W

Dropping the first 4 from W is equivalent to taking the last 2 from W

Drop the last 4 from W

Drop the last 6 of W

Drop and take work with literals too.

A program using DROP ↓

```
      ∇TRI N
[1]   N              ——— print the value of N
[2]   N ← 1 ↓ N      ——— N becomes 1 "drop" N
[3]   → (0 < ρN) /1 ∇     branch to line 1 if 0 < ρN
                          (if N still has something
                           in it)
```

```
      TRI 'CHEAT'
CHEAT
HEAT
EAT
AT
T
```

Program TRI prints a triangle-shape of whatever you give it for N (here 'CHEAT')

```
      TRI 'ANYTHING'
```

→ TRIangle 'ANYTHING'

```
      5 ? 5
1 3 4 5 2
```

5 numbers are randomly selected from 1 2 3 4 5 <u>without</u> <u>replacement</u> (the numbers are scrambled)

```
      5 ? 5
5 4 1 3 2
```

There are no repeats.

```
      5 ? 5
→
```

"Deal" the integers ⍳5 at random.

```
      'STONE'[I ← 5 ? 5]
NOTES
```

Scrambled letters by indexing

```
      I
→
```

What value for I was required for the above result?

```
      1 ? 5
4
```

1 "deal" 5
(1 random number from ⍳5)

```
      2 ? 5
→
```

2 random numbers from ⍳5

```
      3 ? 5
→
```

3 random numbers from ⍳5

```
      4 ? 5
5 1 4 2
```

4 random numbers from ⍳5

```
      5 ? 5
→
```

5 random numbers from ⍳5

A simulated deal of a deck of cards

```
      52 ? 52
43 47 13 7 49 14 25 26 12 19 30 17 48 44 36 35 22 20 18 2 4
      40 33 31 9 28 37 39 1 52 6 42 11 10 27 46 41 45 51 38
      8 29 16 5 34 15 3 23 32 50 24 21
```

(A bridge "hand")

```
      13 ? 52
25 45 43 41 30 48 40 5 17 42 44 10 29
```

```
      13 ? 52
```

(A different "hand")

→

```
      13 ? 13
```

13 "dealt" out of 13

→

```
      14 ? 13
```

14 "dealt" out of 13 (guess)

→

Challenge:

```
      'NOTES'[I[I ← 5 ? 5]]
STENO

      I
```

→

What must I have been for the above to happen?

```
      ⎕ ← PER ← ⍳⍴I
```

→

Repeated indexing producing permutations

```
      ⎕ ← PER ← PER[I]
```

→

```
      ⎕ ← PER ← PER [I]
```

→

```
      ⎕ ← PER ← PER[I]
```

→

```
      ⎕ ← PER ← PER[I]
```

→

```
      ⎕ ← PER ← PER[I]
1 2 3 4 5
```

It comes back to itself!

THE GRADE-UP FUNCTION ⍋

```
      I
3 1 5 2 4

      D1 ← ¯1 7 ¯4 8 2
      D1[I]
¯4 ¯1 2 7 8

      ⍋D1
3 1 5 2 4

      D1[⍋D1]
¯4 ¯1 2 7 8
```

I is a "permutation vector" which happens to sort D1 into <u>ascending</u> order.

The grade-up function ⍋ can be used to produce the same result.

overstrike Δ and |

```
      D2 ← 6 9 ¯2 2 0 7
      ⍋D2
→

      D2[⍋D2]
→
```

⍋ yields a permutation vector-- which will arrange a vector in order

The ascending order of D2

```
      ∇Z ← SORT X
[1]   Z ← X[⍋X] ∇

      SORT V ← 5 13.2 ¯4 9 7 0 3.5
¯4 0 3.5 5 7 9 13.2

      SORT V[(⍴V) ? ⍴V]
→
```

A concise program to SORT any numerical vector into ascending order

SORT scrambled V

```
      D2
6 9 ¯2 2 0 7
```

overstrike ∇ and |

```
      ⍒D2
2 6 1 4 5 3
```

⍒ produces a permutation vector for descending order

```
      D2[⍒D2]
```

→ Arrange D2 in descending order

```
      ⍒6 5 7 8 9
```

→ What are the indices which will arrange these in descending order?

```
      N ← 7 ? 7
      S ← 'NEPTUNE' [N]
      S
```

Suppose N is some permutation vector

→ S is 'NEPTUNE' scrambled

```
      S[⍋N]
```

→ S can be unscrambled by using grade-up ⍋.

```
      N ← 7 ? 7
      S ← 'NEPTUNE' [N]
      S [⍋N]
```

Try it again.

→

THE INDEX-OF FUNCTION ⍳

```
      ALPHABET
ABCDEFGHIJKLMNOPQRSTUVWXYZ

      ALPHABET ⍳ 'A'
1
```

⍳ (used dyadically) yields the index-of 'A' in ALPHABET

```
      ALPHABET ⍳ 'BAT'
2 1 20
```

'B' is the 2nd letter in ALPHABET
'A' is the 1st letter in ALPHABET
'T' is the 20th letter in ALPHABET

```
      ALPHABET ⍳ 'MAN'
→
```

What are the indices of 'M' and 'A' and 'N' in ALPHABET?

```
      ALPHABET ⍳ 'ROBIN'
18 15 2 9 14

      ALPHABET[18 15 2 9 14]
→
```

If you use the indices with ALPHABET, you get . . . ?

```
      ALPHABET ⍳'.'
27
```

In case the value on the right is not found in the values on the left, index-of gives 1+ the number of values on the left.

```
      1 + ⍴ALPHABET
→

      20 16 12 8 8 6 ⍳ 8
4
```

In case of duplicates, index-of only gives the first index.

```
     ∇Z ← LSORT X
[1]  Z ← X [⍋ ALPHABET ⍳ X]
     ∇
```

Program LSORT will sort literals into alphabetic order

```
     LSORT 'CAT'
ACT

     LSORT 'SLOT'
```

→

INDEX ORIGIN — A SYSTEM VARIABLE ⎕IO

```
      ⎕IO ← 0
```

This command changes the origin of indices from 1 to 0
It affects the deal function,

```
      5 ? 5
4 0 3 1 2
```

the index-generator,

```
      ⍳8
0 1 2 3 4 5 6 7
```

the index-of function

```
      'ZERO' ⍳ 'ONE'
3 4 1
```

as well as all indexing operations (see also: pp. 129, 131, chapter 8)

```
      'ZERO'[2]
R
```

and grade-up

```
      ⍋6 9 ¯2 2 0 7
→
```

and grade-down

```
      ⍒6 9 ¯2 2 0 7
→
```

The command to change the origin back to 1.

```
      ⎕IO ← 1
```

Normal execution

```
      5 ? 5
2 3 1 4 5

      ⍳8
→

      'ZERO'[2]
→
```

Note: ⎕IO is one of several "system variables" all of which begin with ⎕. See 214!

REVIEW

APL has a rich resource of *functions*—you may consider them "tools"—to *apply* in programming. The random number generator ? , for example, is convenient for simulating real-world processes, experiments, and, of course, games. Other useful functions include: membership ∊ , take ↑ , drop ↓ , deal ? , grade-up ⍋ , grade-down ⍒ , and index-of ⍳ .

Programs may have several local names (in addition to those needed for syntax). They are listed following semicolons in the program's header and are used to keep track of values—such as in counters—which are only needed while the program is being executed. In fact, all local names lose their values after execution is completed.

Programs may have sub-programs. (And sub-programs may have sub-programs, etc.) They may be used within expressions, but only with the proper syntax. A main program continues execution exactly where it left off after a sub-program is completed.

Some system variables affect certain APL functions. ⎕*IO* is one such system variable which acts to change the index origin.

change the index origin.

To test your understanding of U-Program 5, begin writing programs of your own choosing using these tools. See U-Program 6 for examples.

U-Program 6

INTERACTIVE PROGRAMS

Contents

```
      3 × ⎕
⎕:
      7
21

      A ← ⎕
⎕:
      5
      A
5

      B ← ⎕
⎕:
      9
      B
→

      C ← 4 × ⎕
⎕:
      8
      C
32

      N ← ⎕
⎕:
      17 × 2
      N
→
```

⎕ (the "quad" symbol) requests input. The computer prints ⎕: and then waits.

You must enter a number before 3 × ⎕ can be evaluated (← 7)

Requesting input for A

You enter 5 (← 5)

A is now 5

Requesting input for B

9 is entered

What is the value of B?

C is 4 times the "quad" (to be some number)

8 is entered for the quad

Then C is 32

N is to be some thing

Evaluate this.

N is that number

```
      S ← ⎕
⎕:
      3 ∪ 4
SYNTAX ERROR
      3∪4
        ∧
⎕:
```

If you enter an improper expression (one which produces an error report), the request for input is repeated.

```
      →
```

If you enter a right-pointing arrow → (an empty branch), the request is terminated.

```
      S
VALUE ERROR
      S
      ∧
```

And S will not have a value

Challenge:

```
      5 × 8 ⌈ ⎕ + 2
⎕:
      10
60
```

With 10 in place of ⎕ the expression evaluates to be 60.

```
      5 × 8 ⌈ ⎕ + 2
⎕:
      7
→
```

What is the evaluation of the expression for 7 in place of ⎕ ?

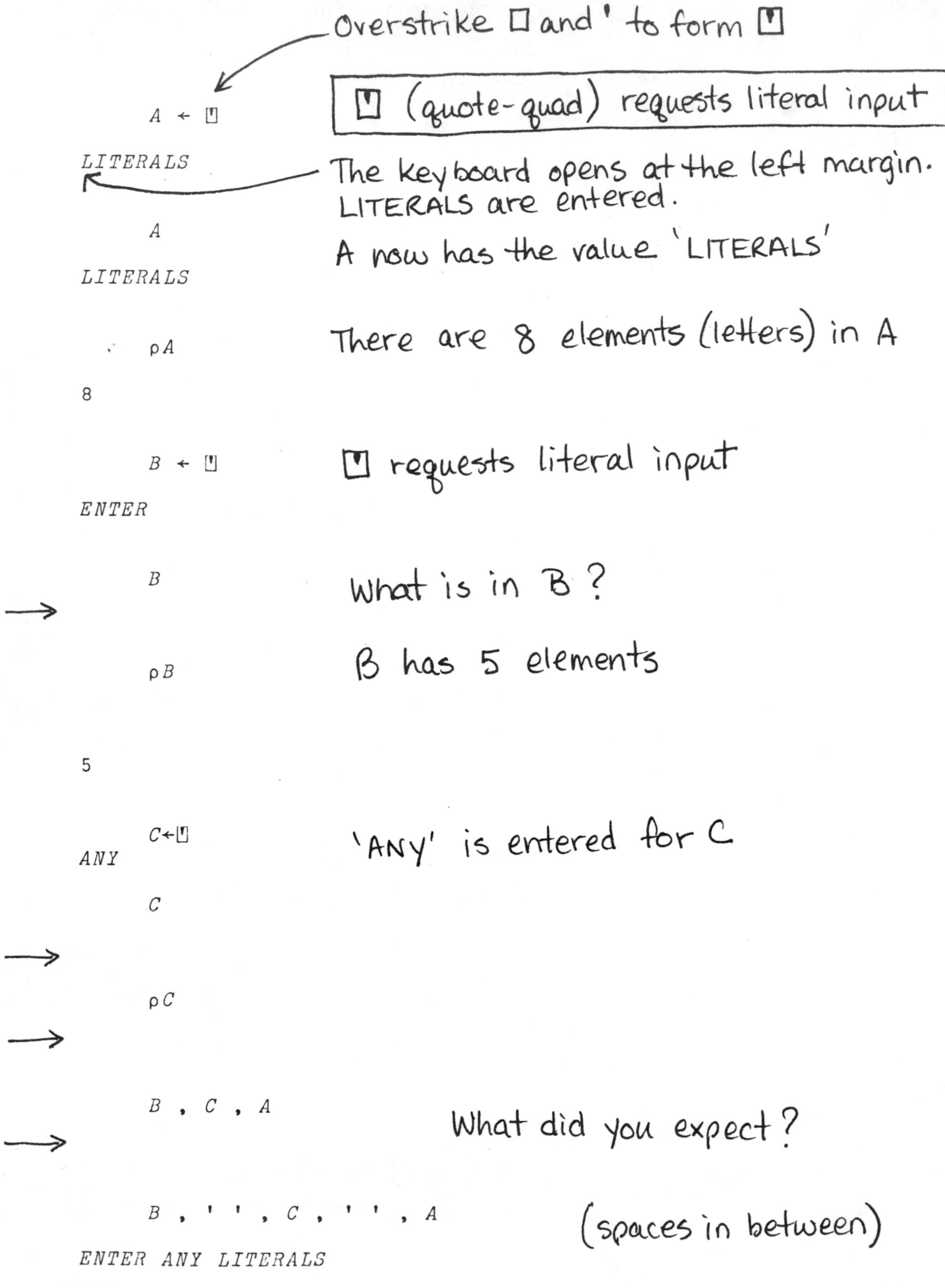
Overstrike ⎕ and ' to form ⍞
A ← ⍞
⍞ (quote-quad) requests literal input
LITERALS
The keyboard opens at the left margin. LITERALS are entered.
A
A now has the value 'LITERALS'
LITERALS
ρA
There are 8 elements (letters) in A
8
B ← ⍞
⍞ requests literal input
ENTER
B
What is in B ?
→
ρB
B has 5 elements
5
C←⍞
ANY
'ANY' is entered for C
C
→
ρC
→
B , C , A
What did you expect?
→
B , ' ' , C , ' ' , A
(spaces in between)
ENTER ANY LITERALS

```
      X ← 'TYLENE'

      X ← ⍞ , X
ACE

      X
```

'ACE' goes where ⍞ is

Then, what is the value of X?

```
      Y ← ⍞
```

O backspace U backspace T

```
      ⍴Y
VALUE ERROR
      ⍴Y
       ∧
```

This "satisfies" the request for literal input... but Y does not have a value.

```
    ∇DRILL
[1] 'MULTIPLY'
[2] X ← ? 20                ——— X is a random number from 1 to 20
[3] X
[4] Y ← ? 20                ——— Y is a random number from 1 to 20
[5] Y
[6] ANSWER ← ⎕              ——— accept the student's answer
[7] →(ANSWER = X × Y) / 1   ——— if his ANSWER is correct, go to line 1 (and give another problem) otherwise, print NO, TRY AGAIN and then go back to line 6.
[8] 'NO, TRY AGAIN'
[9] →6 ∇
```

Execution of program DRILL

```
    DRILL
MULTIPLY
16
11
⎕:
    176

MULTIPLY
14
13
⎕:
    143
NO, TRY AGAIN
⎕:
    272
NO, TRY AGAIN
⎕:
    182
```

There's a problem with this program

```
MULTIPLY
11
4
⎕:
      44
MULTIPLY
18
3
⎕:
      →
```

:

the student has no way to stop it!

(If he gets a problem correct, he is given another one; if he makes a mistake, he is given another try. This will go on and on . . .)

unless → is entered

```
      ∇DRILL[6.5] →(ANSWER=STOP)/0∇
```

Let's insert a line which permits the student to stop the program.

```
      STOP←99.9
```

STOP is assigned some number not likely to be a response to these multiplication problems

```
      DRILL
MULTIPLY
10
1
⎕:
      10
MULTIPLY
17
10
⎕:
      1170
NO, TRY AGAIN
⎕:
      STOP
```

When the student enters STOP, the program is terminated.

```
      ∇DRILL[⎕]∇

    ∇ DRILL
[1]   'MULTIPLY'
[2]   X←?20
[3]   X
[4]   Y←?20
[5]   Y
[6]   ANSWER←⎕
[7]   →(ANSWER=STOP)/0
[8]   →(ANSWER=X×Y)/1
[9]   'NO, TRY AGAIN'
[10]  →6
    ∇
```

The current definition of DRILL

LINE EDITING

-- allowing you to change single characters on a line --

```
      ∇DRILL[8⎕21]
[8]   →(ANSWER=X×Y)/1
                     /
[8]   →(ANSWER=X×Y)/NEWPROB
[9]   [1⎕7]
[1]   'MULTIPLY'
      8
[1]   NEWPROB:'MULTIPLY'
[2]   [6⎕7]
[6]   ANSWER←⎕
      6
[6]   GUESS:ANSWER←⎕
[7]   [10] →GUESS∇
```

this elides the character 1

then you type in new characters NEWPROB

this will place 8 spaces in front of 'MULTIPLY'

where you type in new characters

The general form of line editing is

∇ program name [n ⎕ m]

where n ≡ line number
and m ≡ number of spaces from left margin to position the type ball

The new definition of DRILL

```
      ∇DRILL[⎕]∇

    ∇ DRILL
[1]  NEWPROB:'MULTIPLY'
[2]    X←?20
[3]    X
[4]    Y←?20
[5]    Y
[6]  GUESS:ANSWER←⎕
[7]    →(ANSWER=STOP)/0
[8]    →(ANSWER=X×Y)/NEWPROB
[9]    'NO, TRY AGAIN'
[10]   →GUESS
    ∇
```

LINE LABELS

NEWPROB and GUESS are line labels.
Line labels are names followed by a colon and an expression on a line in a program.

They take on the value of the line number and may be used for convenience in branching.

```
      DRILL
MULTIPLY
13
9
⎕:
      STOP


      NEWPROB
VALUE ERROR
      NEWPROB
      ^


      GUESS
VALUE ERROR
      GUESS
      ^
```

Line labels are <u>local</u> to the program;

that is, they have no values after completion of the program.

You may, therefore, safely use the same line labels in different programs without interference.

Refinements to DRILL

Now we will change DRILL to display multiplication problems in a different way.

```
      ∇DRILL[1⎕]                          display line [1]
[1]   NEWPROB:'MULTIPLY'
[1]    NEWPROB:'    ';X←?99               change line [1]
[2]                                       delete line [2]     (push ATTN key)

[3]    'x  ';Y←?99                        change line [3]
[4]    4ρ'¯'                              change line [4]
[5]                                       delete line [5]     (push ATTN key)

[6]    ∇
```

(All other lines remain the same)

see p. 120

```
      ∇DRILL[⎕]∇

    ∇ DRILL
[1]   NEWPROB:'    ';X←?99
[2]    'x  ';Y←?99
[3]    4ρ'¯'
[4]   GUESS:ANSWER←⎕
[5]    →(ANSWER=STOP)/0
[6]    →(ANSWER=X×Y)/NEWPROB
[7]    'NO, TRY AGAIN'
[8]    →GUESS
    ∇
```

This is what DRILL looks like now

; is used for mixed output -- that is, when you want to print out numerical and literal data on the same line. (See lines [1] and [2] of DRILL)

```
      DRILL

  42
× 30
----

⎕:
      1260

  74
× 89
----

⎕:
      STOP
```

Multiplication problems in a new format

Further refinements to DRILL

Editing DRILL to keep track of the total number of problems completed correctly (N) and the number of consecutive wrong answers (W).

```
      ∇DRILL[0⎕]
[0]    DRILL
[0]    DRILL;N;W
[1]    [.5] N←0
[0.6]  NEWPROB:W←0
[0.7]  N←N+1
[0.8]  →(N>5)/END
[0.9]  [1⎕6]
[1]   NEWPROB:'   ';X←?99
      ////////
[1]    '   ';X←?99
[2]    [7.5] W←W+1
[7.6]  [8⎕8]
[8]    →GUESS
        6
[8]    →(W≤3)/GUESS
[9]    'LATER.  GET SOME HELP NOW!'
[10]   →0
[11]   END: 'THAT''S ALL.'∇
```

The revised program

```
      ∇DRILL[⎕]∇

    ∇ DRILL;N;W
[1]    N←0
[2]   NEWPROB:W←0
[3]    N←N+1
[4]    →(N>5)/END
[5]    '   ';X←?99
[6]    '×  ';Y←?99
[7]    4ρ'-'
[8]   GUESS:ANSWER←⎕
[9]    →(ANSWER=STOP)/0
[10]   →(ANSWER=X×Y)/NEWPROB
[11]   'NO, TRY AGAIN'
[12]   W←W+1
[13]   →(W≤3)/GUESS
[14]   'LATER.  GET SOME HELP NOW!'
[15]   →0
[16]  END: 'THAT''S ALL.'
    ∇
```

- [1] initialize N to be 0
- [2] initialize W to be 0
- [3] increment N by 1
- [4] branch to the END (line [16]) after 5 correct problems
- [5]–[7] display the problem
- [8] the student's ANSWER
- [11] if wrong,
- [12] increment W by 1
- [13] branch to GUESS (line [8]) after 3 or fewer repeated wrong answers

(go to line [14] after the 4th wrong answer)

```
      DRILL
```

Execution of DRILL

```
   53
×  22
----

⎕:
      1166
   20
×  93
----

⎕:
      1860
   17
×  71
----

⎕:
      177
NO, TRY AGAIN
⎕:
      1207
   18
×  41
----

⎕:
      738
   60
×  50
----

⎕:
      3000
THAT'S ALL.
```

Terminates automatically after 5 problems are completed correctly.

```
      DRILL
   57
×  53
----

⎕:
      1551
NO, TRY AGAIN
⎕:
      2521
NO, TRY AGAIN
⎕:
      2831
NO, TRY AGAIN
⎕:
      2921
NO, TRY AGAIN
LATER.  GET SOME HELP NOW!
```

Terminates automatically after 4 consecutive wrong answers to a problem.

```
      END
→
```

Does line label END have a value now?

a common editing procedure: display a line and then change it.

```
     ∇DRILL[16⎕]
[16] END:'THAT''S ALL.'
[16]  END:'CONGRATULATIONS! WOULD YOU LIKE 5 MORE?'
[17]  'ENTER Y FOR YES, N FOR NO.'
[18]  →('Y'∊⍞)/1
[19]  'O.K.  NO HARD FEELINGS.  SEE YOU NEXT TIME.'∇
```

With these changes,

```
     DRILL
```

You execute the program

→

—— after getting 5 right, try entering Y or YES or ANYTHING

```
      ∇DRILL [17⎕14]
[17]   'ENTER Y FOR YES, N FOR NO.'
              //////    /// /
[17]   'ENTER YES OR NO.'
[18]   [18⎕10]
[18]   →('Y'∊⍞)/1
           2/1
[18]   →('YES'=⍞)/1
[19]   ∇
```

When you line edit here, ∊ is elided, then you type in the ES and = .

```
      DRILL
   90
×  62
----

⍞:
      90 × 62
   84
×  39
----

⎕:
      84 × 39
   67
×  51
----

⎕:
      67 × 51
   49
×  69
----

⎕:
      X × Y
   32
×  18
----

⎕:
      X × Y
CONGRATULATIONS! WOULD YOU LIKE 5 MORE?
ENTER YES OR NO
NO
LENGTH ERROR
DRILL[18] →('YES'=⍞)/1
                 ^
```

Hey, You Cheat!!

Obviously, there's a "flaw" in this design... (⍞ could be used to handle this.)

This error suspends the program (LENGTH ERROR results because the length (size) of 'YES' is not the same as 'NO'.)

```
      )SI
DRILL[18] *
```

This State Indicator command indicates that program DRILL is suspended on line [18].

SUSPENDED PROGRAM

```
      )SI
DRILL[18] *
```

When a program is suspended, its execution has been halted before completion.

```
      N
6
```

The values of local names are available,

```
      W
0

      GUESS
8
```

and line labels too.

```
      NEWPROB
2

      END
16
```

Most importantly, a suspended program may be <u>resumed</u> later-- perhaps after correcting error(s)-- by typing a branch command, e.g. → 18

```
      )SI
DRILL[18] *
```

To clear a program from a state of suspension,

```
      →
```

enter a right-pointing arrow → (one for each suspension *).

```
      )SI
```

Now the state indicator is empty,

```
      W
VALUE ERROR
      W
      ^
```

and local variables do not have values available.

Note: The state indicator is helpful in keeping track of the status of programs as you execute them.

The current definition of DRILL

```
      ∇DRILL[⎕]∇
    ∇ DRILL;N;W
[1]    N←0
[2]   NEWPROB:W←0
[3]    N←N+1
[4]    →(N>5)/END
[5]    '   ';X←?99
[6]    '× ';Y←?99
[7]    4ρ'-'
[8]   GUESS:ANSWER←⎕
[9]    →(ANSWER=STOP)/0
[10]   →(ANSWER=X×Y)/NEWPROB
[11]   'NO, TRY AGAIN'
[12]   W←W+1
[13]   →(W≤3)/GUESS
[14]   'LATER.  GET SOME HELP NOW!'
[15]   →0
[16]  END:'CONGRATULATIONS! WOULD YOU LIKE 5 MORE?'
[17]   'ENTER YES OR NO.'
[18]   →('YES'=⍞)/1
[19]   'O.K.  NO HARD FEELINGS. SEE YOU NEXT TIME.'
    ∇
```

Challenge:

```
      ∇DRILL[18]
```

DRILL may be edited to rectify the problem which caused the previous suspension.

→

```
      DRILL
```

Then execute DRILL.

→

```
    ∇ LOL
[1]    'WELCOME TO THE GAME OF LAST-ONE LOSES!'
[2]    ''
[3]    'DO YOU KNOW THE RULES?'
[4]    →L1×⍳'Y'∊⍞
[5]    RULES
[6]   L1:'TO START WITH THERE ARE ';N←5+?10;' BOXES'
[7]    (2×N)⍴'⎕ '
[8]    'WANT TO GO FIRST OR SECOND?'
[9]    →L2×⍳'F'∊⍞
[10]  L3:'MY MOVE.'
[11]   N←N-MMOVE
[12]   (2×N)⍴'⎕ '
[13]   →WIN×⍳N=1
[14]   →LOSE×⍳N=0
[15]  L2:'YOUR MOVE.'
[16]   N←N-PMOVE
[17]   →LOSE×⍳N=1
[18]   →WIN×⍳N≤0
[19]   (2×N)⍴'⎕ '
[20]   →L3
[21]  WIN:'I WIN THIS TIME.'
[22]   →L4
[23]  LOSE:'RATFINK!!!  YOU WIN.'
[24]  L4:'TYPE  LOL  TO PLAY AGAIN.'
    ∇
```

LAST-ONE-LOSES is a variant of the ancient intellectual game, NIM

LOL is the main program.

Note the use of null literal '' on line [2], line labels on lines [6], [10], [15], [21], [23], and [24], a different branching format on lines [4], [9], [13], [14], etc., and the use of sub-programs.

RULES is a sub-program (self-explanatory)

```
    ∇ RULES
[1]    ''
[2]    'LAST-ONE-LOSES IS A GAME OF TAKING AWAY BOXES.'
[3]    'WHEN IT IS YOUR TURN, YOU MAY TAKE 1 2 OR 3 BOXES.'
[4]    'YOU AND THE COMPUTER WILL TAKE TURNS TAKING BOXES AWAY'
[5]    'UNTIL THERE IS ONLY ONE BOX LEFT.  WHOEVER TAKES THE'
[6]    'LAST ONE LOSES!'
[7]    ''
    ∇
```

PMOVE is a sub-program which accepts the player's move. Note that it checks to be sure a 1 2 or 3 is entered.

```
    ∇ Z←PMOVE
[1]    Z←⎕
[2]    →0×⍳Z∊⍳3
[3]    'PLEASE ENTER A 1 2 OR 3'
[4]    →1
    ∇
```

MMOVE is a sub-program which makes the computer's move. The move is simply a random number from 1 to 3, but less than or equal to N, the number of boxes. (Considerably more sophisticated strategies could be programmed here)

```
    ∇ Z←MMOVE
[1]    Z←N⌊?3
    ∇
```

A sample game.

```
      LOL

WELCOME TO THE GAME OF LAST-ONE-LOSES!

DO YOU KNOW THE RULES?
NOPE

LAST-ONE-LOSES IS A GAME OF TAKING AWAY BOXES.
WHEN IT IS YOUR TURN, YOU MAY TAKE 1 2 OR 3 BOXES.
YOU AND THE COMPUTER WILL TAKE TURNS TAKING BOXES AWAY
UNTIL THERE IS ONLY ONE BOX LEFT.  WHOEVER TAKES THE
LAST ONE LOSES!

TO START WITH THERE ARE 13 BOXES
⎕ ⎕ ⎕ ⎕ ⎕ ⎕ ⎕ ⎕ ⎕ ⎕ ⎕ ⎕ ⎕
WANT TO GO FIRST OR SECOND?

FIRST
YOUR MOVE.
⎕:
      2
⎕ ⎕ ⎕ ⎕ ⎕ ⎕ ⎕ ⎕ ⎕ ⎕ ⎕
MY MOVE.
⎕ ⎕ ⎕ ⎕ ⎕ ⎕ ⎕ ⎕
YOUR MOVE.
⎕:
      3
⎕ ⎕ ⎕ ⎕ ⎕
MY MOVE.
⎕ ⎕ ⎕
YOUR MOVE.
⎕:
      2
RATFINK!!!  YOU WIN.
TYPE  LOL  TO PLAY AGAIN.
```

Playing again.

```
      LOL

WELCOME TO THE GAME OF LAST-ONE-LOSES!

DO YOU KNOW THE RULES?
YES
TO START WITH THERE ARE 6 BOXES
⎕ ⎕ ⎕ ⎕ ⎕ ⎕
WANT TO GO FIRST OR SECOND?

SECOND
MY MOVE.
⎕ ⎕ ⎕ ⎕ ⎕
YOUR MOVE.
⎕:
      1
⎕ ⎕ ⎕ ⎕
MY MOVE.
⎕
I WIN THIS TIME.
TYPE  LOL  TO PLAY AGAIN.
```

Lucky computer!

```
     ∇TEMPER
[1]   EMOTION←0
[2]   'HOW DO YOU FEEL ABOUT ME?'
[3]  ENTER:NEW←⎕
[4]   EMOTION←NEW+EMOTION÷2
[5]   →(EMOTION>10)/MAD
[6]   →ENTER
[7]  MAD:'**!?!*!?'
     ∇
```

TEMPER is a program which simulates -- albeit crudely -- an emotional reaction.

This program will -- under certain conditions -- "get mad at you"!

```
      TEMPER
HOW DO YOU FEEL ABOUT ME?
⎕:
      4
⎕:
      6
⎕:
      8
**!?!*!?
```

It begins by asking you to express how you feel toward the program. Numbers are used to indicate the strength of your feelings: low numbers are very kind or loving, high numbers are hostile or frustrating.

You may ENTER a sequence of NEW numbers -- one at a time. Each number causes EMOTION to be changed according to a simple mathematical model:
EMOTION becomes the NEW value plus one half the previous value of EMOTION.

If EMOTION ever becomes greater than 10, the program goes to MAD (where the computer's vernacular is printed)

```
      TEMPER
→
```

Try different sequences (like 8 6 4 or 8 4 6 or 7 2 7 or 2 7 7, etc.)

```
      TEMPER

HOW DO YOU FEEL ABOUT ME?
□:

      5

□:

      5

□:

      5

□:

      5

□:

      5

□:

      5

□:

      5

□:

      5

□:
```

→

How many 5's do you think this program can "tolerate"?

REVIEW

Interactive programs permit you to enter data during their execution. In APL, the quad ⎕ and quote-quad ⍞ symbols are used to request input—the latter accepting only literal input.

A drill-and-practice program is one which interacts with a student in order to improve his skills, say in multiplication. A prototype of such a program would give directions, present problems, request the student's answers, and judge the answers for correctness. Based on whether an answer is right or wrong, the program branches and gives the appropriate response.

Line editing allows you to change single characters on a line in a program and is helpful in refining a program after it has been defined. Line labels are particularly convenient when a program is to undergo further editing changes. A line label is local to a program and takes on the value of the line number with which it is currently associated. Hence, even after new lines have been inserted or deleted, branching commands using line labels will still be valid.

When a program is executed and produces an error, it is said to be "suspended." The remainder of the program—not yet completed—is temporarily held in abeyance. By checking the "state indicator")*SI* , you can find out where, when, and how many suspensions have occurred. Execution can be resumed with a branch command.

A game is ideal for writing as an interactive program, especially one in which a player competes against the computer. Strategies for making the computer's moves can be programmed, perhaps the simplest of which is by random selection.

A simulation is an approximation of some real-world phenomenon. Simulating something as complex as human behavior is extremely challenging, although simple mathematical models can be expressed easily in APL.

U-Program 7

ARRAYS

Contents

```
      5 ρ 3
3 3 3 3 3
```

(This is the dyadic use of the rho symbol ρ)
5ρ3 generates an array of 5 3's (a "vector")

```
      5 ρ 4
4 4 4 4 4
```

5 4's

```
      4 ρ 5
5 5 5 5
```

4 5's

```
      3 ρ 5
```

→

3 5's

Generally the form is: (structure) ρ (elements)

```
      7 ρ 8 9
8 9 8 9 8 9 8
```

```
      6 ρ 8 9 10
```

→

When there are toofew elements, repeat them until the structure is filled up.

```
      5 ρ 8 9 10 11
8 9 10 11 8
```

```
      4 ρ 8 9 10 11 12
8 9 10 11
```

```
      3 ρ 8 9 10 11 12 13
```

→

When there are too many, use only enough elements to fill the structure.

MATRICES

```
      3 4 ρ 5
5 5 5 5
5 5 5 5
5 5 5 5
```

With two numbers on the left, the array produced is two-dimensional. (a "matrix")

Here, 3 rows and 4 columns of 5's

```
      4 3 ρ 8
8 8 8
8 8 8
8 8 8
8 8 8
```

4 rows 3 columns of 8's

```
      3 5 ρ 2
```

→

3 rows 5 columns of 2's

```
      5 2 ρ 0 0 0 1 1 0 1 1 0 0
0 0
0 1
1 0
1 1
0 0
```

5 by 2 structure, 0s and 1s as elements fill up the matrix, row by row (restructuring a vector into a matrix)

```
      2 5 ρ ι10
```

→

2 rows 5 columns of the elements 1 2 3 4 ... 10

More examples of numerical matrices:

```
      2 3 ρ 1 2
1 2 1
2 1 2
```

Note that the rows are filled up one at a time.

(This is called "row-major" order)

```
      3 3 ρ 1 0 0 0
```

→

```
      2 3 ρ ι11
1 2 3
4 5 6
```

Dyadic ρ with literals:

```
      5 ρ '-'
-----
```

5 dashes

```
      4 ρ '.'
....
```

4 dots

```
      3 ρ '*'
→
```

3 stars

```
      20 ρ '⎕*'
⎕*⎕*⎕*⎕*⎕*⎕*⎕*⎕*⎕*⎕*
```

A total of 20 symbols, alternating ⎕s and *s.

```
      7 ρ 'TOOT'
→
```

A total of 7 elements, repeating when necessary

```
      5 ρ 'PHOTOGRAPHY'
PHOTO
```

The first 5 elements

```
      3 ρ 'SEXTUPLE'
→
```

The first 3

```
      12 ρ 'OH! '
→
```

12 elements in total

! is an overstrike symbol
Type ' backspace .

```
      3 4 ρ 'FREEFROMDEBT'
FREE
FROM
DEBT
```

A 3 by 4 literal matrix

```
      2 30 ρ 'AND MILES TO GO BEFORE I SLEEP'
```

→

2 by 30 (repeat 30 characters)

```
      6 3 ρ 'TO BE OR NOT'
```

→

Repeat in order to fill up 6 by 3 matrix

```
      L ← 3 4 ρ 'GOODPLAYBILL'
      L
```

→

L is specified to be a matrix of 3 rows and 4 columns

```
      ρL
3 4
```

ρL (monadic) gives the structure of L -- 3 rows, 4 columns

```
      ,L
GOODPLAYBILL
```

THE RAVEL FUNCTION ,

, converts a matrix (or any array) into a vector

```
      M ← 3 4 ρ ι12
```

M is a matrix,

```
      M

1  2  3  4
5  6  7  8
9 10 11 12
```

```
      ρM

3 4
```

its structure is 3 by 4,

and

```
      ,M

1 2 3 4 5 6 7 8 9 10 11 12
```

its elements are ←

```
      ρ,M
```

(How many elements -- total?)

→

```
      M + 1

 2  3  4  5
 6  7  8  9
10 11 12 13
```

You may perform functions on M in an element-by-element fashion.

```
      M × 3
```

→

Each element of M times 3

```
      (,M) = (×/ρM)ρM
```

→

Try these functions with MATRIX

```
MATRIX ← 3 4 ρ 9 5 0 6 2 4 11 3 16 8 20 7
MATRIX
```

→

```
ρMATRIX
```

→

```
,MATRIX
```

→

```
MATRIX - 2
```

→

```
6 ⌈ MATRIX
```

→

```
MATRIX = 3
```

→

```
3 ∊ MATRIX
```

→

```
MATRIX ∊ 3
```

→

ARRAY INDEXING

```
      ⎕ ← MATRIX ← 3 4 ⍴ 9 5 0 6 2 4 11 3 16 8 20 7
 9 5  0 6
 2 4 11 3
16 8 20 7
```

Specifying and displaying MATRIX

```
      MATRIX[2;3]
11
```

Indexing the 2nd row, 3rd column of MATRIX

```
      MATRIX[1;4]
6
```

The 1st row, 4th column element

```
      MATRIX[3;2]
→
```

The 3rd row, 2nd column element

```
      MATRIX[1;]
9 5 0 6
```

The 1st row (and all columns)

```
      MATRIX[;3]
0 11 20
```

The 3rd column (and all rows) (printed as a vector)

```
      MATRIX[3;]
→
```

The 3rd row

```
      MATRIX[;2]
→
```

The 2nd column

```
MATRIX[;2 4]
```

The 2nd and 4th columns

```
5 6
4 3
8 7
```

```
MATRIX[2 3;2 4]
```

The 2nd and 3rd row elements of the 2nd and 4th columns

```
4 3
8 7
```

```
MATRIX[2;4 2 3]
```

2nd row; 4th, 2nd and 3rd columns

→

```
MATRIX[3 2 3;3]
```

3rd, 2nd, and 3rd rows of 3rd column

→

Challenge:

```
MATRIX[1 2 3;1 2 3]=MATRIX[2;2]
```

→

There will be 9 answers to this-- in a 3 by 3 matrix

Challenge:

```
I ← ρMATRIX

MATRIX[I[1];I[2]]
```

→

```
MATRIX[;ιI[2]]=MATRIX[ιI[1];]
```

→

REDUCTION WITH ARRAYS

```
      ⎕ ← MAT ← 2 3 ⍴ ⍳6
1 2 3
4 5 6
```

MAT has two dimensions (rows and columns)

```
      +/[1] MAT
5 7 9
```

The sum-reduction of the first dimension of MAT (adding down the columns)

```
      +/[2] MAT
6 15
```

The sum-reduction of the second dimension of MAT (adding across the rows)

```
      (+/MAT)=+/[2]MAT
1 1
```

+/MAT is an abbreviated way of writing +/[2] MAT

```
      +/MAT
→
```

(The last dimension is understood)

```
      (+⌿MAT)=+/[1]MAT
1 1 1
```

+⌿ is the abbreviation for +/[1] (adding vertically)

```
      +⌿MAT
→
```

(The first dimension is understood)

```
      +/+/MAT
21
```

Adding up all the elements

```
      +/,MAT
→
```

```
      MAT
1 2 3
4 5 6
```

The product-reduction of MAT

```
      ×⌿MAT
4 10 18
```

```
      ×/MAT
```

→

Difference-reduction

```
      -⌿MAT
```

→

```
      -/MAT
2 5
```

(1-2-3) , (4-5-6)

```
      (+/+/MAT) = -/-/MAT
```

Is this true?

→

```
      (1 × 3 × 5 ÷ 2 × 4 × 6) = ÷/,MAT
```

(1 ÷ 2 ÷ 3 ÷ 4 ÷ 5 ÷ 6)

→

THE COMPRESSION FUNCTION APPLIED TO ARRAYS

```
      0 1 0  ⌿  3 3 ρ ⍳9
4 5 6
```

0 1 0 is compressed on the rows (the first dimension)

```
      0 1 0 / 3 3 ρ ⍳9
2
5
8
```

0 1 0 is compressed on the columns (the last dimension)

```
      ⎕ ← M ← 4 4 ρ 'SOLDOHIOFINETOES'
SOLD
OHIO
FINE
TOES
```

```
      L ← 1 1 0 0
      K ← 1 0 1 0
```

```
      L⌿M
```

Compress the rows

→

```
      K/M
```

Compress the columns

→

Take ↑ and Drop ↓ applied to matrices:

```
      ⎕ ← MATE ← 3 4 ρ 'JIBEFORESAIL'
JIBE
FORE
SAIL
```

A literal matrix, MATE

```
      2 3 ↑ MATE
JIB
FOR
```

Take the first 2 rows and the first 3 columns.

```
      ¯2 ¯3 ↑ MATE
ORE
AIL
```

Take the last 2 rows and the last 3 columns.

```
      3 ¯1 ↑ MATE
→
```

Take the first 3 rows and the last 1 column.

```
      2 3 ↓ MATE
L
```

Drop the first 2 rows and the first 3 columns.

```
      2 1 ↓ MATE
→
```

Drop the first 2 rows and the first 1 column.

SUMMARY OF APL DATA STRUCTURES

```
      ⎕ ← S ← 14
14
```

S is a scalar (no dimension)

```
      ⎕ ← V ← 2 3 5 7 11 13
2 3 5 7 11 13
```

V is a vector (one dimension)

```
      ⎕ ← M ← 3 4 ρ ι12
1  2  3  4
5  6  7  8
9 10 11 12
```

M is a matrix (two-dimensional)

```
      ⎕ ← H ← 3 2 4 ρ 7
7 7 7 7
7 7 7 7

7 7 7 7
7 7 7 7

7 7 7 7
7 7 7 7
```

H is a 3-array (three-dimensional)

4-arrays
5-arrays
etc.
are allowed too

ρ of an array is its "structure"

```
      ρH
3 2 4
```
H has 3 planes of 2 rows 4 columns

```
      ρM
3 4
```
M has 3 rows and 4 columns

```
      ρV
6
```
V has 6 elements (columns)

```
      ρS

```
S has no structure

← (blank line)

ρρ of an array is its "rank" (how many dimensions)

```
      ρρH
3
```
H is a 3-array

```
      ρρM
2
```
M is a 2-array (matrix)

```
      ρρV
1
```
V is a 1-array (vector)

```
      ρρS
0
```
S is a 0-array (scalar)

```
ALPHABET ← 'ABCDEFGHIJKLMNOPQRSTUVWXYZ'
```

RANDOM is a program which prints N randomly generated "words" with a certain number of LETTERS.

```
∇N RANDOM LETTERS;J

[1]   J←0
[2]   ALPHABET[?LETTERSρ26]
[3]   J←J+1
[4]   →(J<N)/2∇
```

LETTERS ρ 26 generates an array of 26's which are then used as random indices of the ALPHABET. J is a local name used to count up to N.

```
7 RANDOM 3

QFA
RKG
LGC
DZT
KLN
DKD
NSA
```

7 randomly generated 3-letter "words"

```
3 RANDOM 7
```

→

3 random 7-letter "words"

```
ALPHABET[? 3 7 ρ 26]

BNQDZUP
RVBMATT
KJCJEXL
```

A more direct way to produce the same result, using a matrix index.

```
    ∇ SPELLING
[1]    'SPELL';Y←?8
[2]    X←⍞
[3]    →0×⍳0=⍴X
[4]    →(∧/W[Y;]=5↑X)/1
[5]    'THE CORRECT SPELLING IS ';W[Y;]
[6]    →1
    ∇
```

Program SPELLING* drills a student in spelling the numbers 1 through 8 (presented randomly).

```
      W ← 8 5 ⍴ 'ONE  TWO  THREEFOUR FIVE SIX  SEVENEIGHT'
```

W is a matrix of the correct spellings

```
      SPELLING

SPELL 7

SEVEN

SPELL 5

FIVE

SPELL 8

ATE

THE CORRECT SPELLING IS EIGHT

SPELL 1

UNITY

THE CORRECT SPELLING IS ONE

SPELL 5

FIVE

SPELL 4

FORE

THE CORRECT SPELLING IS FOUR

SPELL 4

FOURTEEN

THE CORRECT SPELLING IS FOUR

SPELL 8

EIGHTY

SPELL 6
```

Hmmm.

Enter nothing and the program stops.

Program MDRILL* gives a student drill in multiplication with hints. Note that line [6] prints a matrix of small circles.

```
     ∇MDRILL N
[1]   Y←?N
[2]   Y[1];' × ';Y[2]
[3]   →0×⍳∧/'STOP'∊A←⎕
[4]   →⍳A=×/Y
[5]   'DUMMY.  LOOK:'
[6]   Yρ'∘'
[7]   'NOW TRY IT.'
[8]   →⍳⎕=×/Y
[9]   'YOU BLEW IT.'
[10]  'THE ANSWER IS ';×/Y
[11]  →1∇
```

15 and 10 are limits for the random numbers

```
      MDRILL 15 10

9 × 3
⎕:
      29
DUMMY. LOOK:
∘∘∘
∘∘∘
∘∘∘
∘∘∘
∘∘∘
∘∘∘
∘∘∘
∘∘∘
∘∘∘
NOW TRY IT.
⎕:
      27
12 × 9
⎕:
      108
3 × 7
⎕:
      37
DUMMY.  LOOK:
∘∘∘∘∘∘∘
∘∘∘∘∘∘∘
∘∘∘∘∘∘∘
NOW TRY IT.
⎕:
      22
YOU BLEW IT.
THE ANSWER IS 21
1 × 4
⎕:
      4
7 × 5
⎕:
      'STOP'
```

Here's a hint (a matrix of small circles)

You get two chances before you are told the answer.

*These programs are quite similar to ones first defined by Kenneth Iverson in his paper "The Role of Computers in Teaching", Queen's University, 1968.

REVIEW

APL treats *arrays* as whole entities. Any array—literal or numerical—may be restructured into another array (of the same type) in any specified size. Many APL functions, such as + - × ÷ ⌈ ⌊ | = ≠ < > ≤ ≥ ⋆ ∧ ∨ ∼ extend to arrays; that is, the function applies to each element of the array, and the result is an array of the same size.

The term "array" includes scalars (single elements), vectors (one-dimensional arrays), matrices (two-dimensional arrays), 3-arrays, 4-arrays, etc. In APL the structure of arrays is always rectangular, and elements fill up the latter dimensions of the structure first. For matrices, this amounts to filling up row-by-row. Data structures in APL are related—as seen by the use of ⍴⍴, the "rank" of an array.

The use of arrays-as-wholes greatly facilitates programming. Many programmers claim that APL array-handling capabilities make problem-solving considerably easier.

U-Program 8

ARRAY FUNCTIONS

Contents

```
      V ← 'EVIL'

      ⌽ V
LIVE
```

⌽ is the reversal function (formed by overstriking ○ and |)
⌽ reverses the elements of a vector.

```
      ⌽ 'NOSLIW'
→
```

Flip it.

```
      ⌽ 'DOCNOTEIDISSENTAFASTNEVERPREVENTSAFATNESSIDIETONCOD'
→
```

(one of the world's longest palindromes)

```
      ⎕ ← M ← 3 4 ⍴ ⍳12
1  2  3  4
5  6  7  8
9 10 11 12
```

⌽ with a matrix

```
      ⌽ M
 4  3  2  1
 8  7  6  5
12 11 10  9
```

Each row is reversed (same as ⌽[2] M)

```
      ⊖ M
9 10 11 12
5  6  7  8
1  2  3  4
```

overstrike ○ and −

Each column is reversed (same as ⌽[1] M)

```
      ⌽⊖M
→
```

Reversals in both dimensions

Note: the function symbol shows the axis of reversal:

⌽ (reversal about a vertical axis)

⊖ (reversal about a horizontal axis)

THE TRANSPOSE FUNCTION ⍉ (MONADIC)

⍉ overstrike ○ and \

```
      M

1  2  3  4
5  6  7  8
9 10 11 12

      ⎕ ← M̲ ← ⍉M

1 5  9
2 6 10
3 7 11
4 8 12
```

Each row is transposed to a column, and each column becomes a row.

```
      (⍴M̲) = ⌽⍴M
```

→ The dimensions of M̲ are compared with the reversed dimensions of M.

```
      ⍉N ← 4 3⍴ 'FOEANDICELEN'
```

→ Form a 4 by 3 matrix (N) and then print the elements transposed so that each row is a column and vice versa.

Note: the function symbol shows the axis of transposition:

⍉ (transpose about the main diagonal)

```
      A ← 3
      B ← 'TENFLAT'
      ⎕ ← R ← A⌽B
FLATTEN
      (⍴R) = ⍴B
```

For vectors:

⌽ Rotated 3 elements from the front of the elements of B to the back

Compare the dimension of the result R with the dimension of B

→

Challenge:

```
      ∧/R = (A - ⍴B) ⌽ B
1
```

← A clue to the use of negative numbers with rotation

```
      ¯1 ⌽ 'TOPS'
```

→

```
      M

 1  2  3  4
 5  6  7  8
 9 10 11 12
```

Rotation works similarly with matrices:

```
      3 ⌽ M

 4 1  2  3
 8 5  6  7
12 9 10 11
```

3 columns rotated from each row (front to back)

```
      2 ⌽ M
```

→

Rotate 2 columns from the front of each row to the back

```
      ¯2 ⊖ M

 5  6  7  8
 9 10 11 12
 1  2  3  4
```

2 rows rotated from each column (bottom to top)

```
      ¯1 ⊖ M
```

→

Rotate 1 row from the bottom to the top of each column

Challenge:

```
      ¯2 ⌽ 1 ⊖ ⍉ 5 2 ⍴ 'UPCLEESAAP'
```

→

You may rotate different numbers of elements from different rows or columns.

```
      M

1  2  3  4
5  6  7  8
9 10 11 12
```

Rotate 1 from the first row
2 from the second row
3 from the third row

```
      1 2 3 ⌽ M

 2 3  4  1
 7 8  5  6
12 9 10 11
```

Rotate 3 from the first column
2 from the second column
-1 from the third column (bottom to top)
1 from the fourth column (top to bottom)

```
      3 2 ¯1 1 ⊖ M

1 10 11  8
5  2  3 12
9  6  7  4
```

```
      2 3 ⌽ 2 5⍴ 'LESTA'
```

→

THE TRANSPOSE FUNCTION ⍉ (DYADIC)

```
      ⎕ ← L ← 5 8 ⍴ 'APL '

APL APL
APL APL
APL APL
APL APL
APL APL
```

```
      ⎕ ← L̲ ← 2 1 ⍉ L

AAAAA
PPPPP
LLLLL

AAAAA
PPPPP
LLLLL
```

Normal transpose
(the 2nd dimension is switched
with the 1st dimension)

```
      (⍉L) = 2 1 ⍉ L

1 1 1 1 1
1 1 1 1 1
1 1 1 1 1
1 1 1 1 1
1 1 1 1 1
1 1 1 1 1
1 1 1 1 1
1 1 1 1 1
```

2 1 ⍉ (matrix) is equivalent
to ⍉ (matrix)

```
      (⍉L̲) = 2 1 ⍉ L̲
```

→

```
      (⍴L̲) = (⍴L)[2 1]
```

→

```
      2 1 ⍉ ⎕ ← SQ ← 4 4 ⍴ ⍳16
 1  2  3  4
 5  6  7  8
 9 10 11 12
13 14 15 16
 1  5  9 13
 2  6 10 14
 3  7 11 15
 4  8 12 16
```

A matrix SQ

Its transpose

1 1 ⍉ (matrix) yields its <u>diagonal</u> elements

```
      ⎕ ← D ← 1 1 ⍉ SQ
1 6 11 16
```

```
      I ← ?4
      D[I] = SQ[I;I]
```

→

```
      (⍴D) = ⌊/⍴SQ
```

→

```
      1 1 ⍉ 3 3 ⍴ 'IRSNBAACM'
```

→ The diagonal of this matrix

A REVIEW OF ARRAY FUNCTIONS

```
      ⎕ ← LM ← 2 2 ρ '∘⋆○⊛'
→

      ⌽LM
→

      ⊖LM
→

      ⌽⊖LM
→

      ⍉LM
→

      ⌽⍉LM
→

      ⍉⌽LM
→

      ⌽⍉⌽LM
→

      1 0 ⌽ LM
→

      0 1 ⊖ LM
→

      1 1 ⍉ LM
→
```

```
      X ← ⍳4
      Y ← ⍳5
```

Outer product is used to create arrays by performing a dyadic function on every pair of elements given on the left and right.

```
      X + Y

LENGTH ERROR
      X + Y
      ∧
```

Normal element-by-element addition is not possible because vectors X and Y are of different lengths.

```
      X ∘.+ Y

2 3 4 5 6
3 4 5 6 7
4 5 6 7 8
5 6 7 8 9
```

Outer product gives all the sums of each element of X with each element of Y -- arranged in a table (matrix).

Other dyadic functions may be used with outer product.

```
      X ∘.× Y
```

→

Fill in this table:

×	1	2	3	4	5
1					
2					
3					
4					

(Rows: X; columns: Y)

```
      X ∘.= Y

1 0 0 0 0
0 1 0 0 0
0 0 1 0 0
0 0 0 1 0
```

=	1	2	3	4	5
1	(1=1)	(1=2)	(1=3)	(1=4)	(1=5)
2	(2=1)	(2=2)	(2=3)	(2=4)	(2=5)
3	(3=1)	(3=2)	(3=3)	(3=4)	(3=5)
4	(4=1)	(4=2)	(4=3)	(4=4)	(4=5)

```
      X
1 2 3 4

      Y
1 2 3 4 5

      X ∘.* Y
1       1       1       1       1
2       4       8      16      32
3       9      27      81     243
4      16      81     256    1024

      ρY ∘.* X
→

      X ∘.⌊ Y
→

      Y ∘.< Y

0 1 1 1 1
0 0 1 1 1
0 0 0 1 1
0 0 0 0 1
0 0 0 0 0
```

The general form of outer product is (array)∘.f(array)

where f is any dyadic function which extends to arrays.

(+ − × ÷ * = < ≤ ≥ > ≠ ⌊ ⌈ | etc.)

Note that the size of the result is (ρX), ρY

⌊	1	2	3	4	5
1					
2					
3					
4					

<	1	2	3	4	5
1	0	1	1	1	1
2	0	0	1	1	1
3	0	0	0	1	1
4	0	0	0	0	1
5	0	0	0	0	0

```
      (⍳10) ∘.× ⍳10
```

The multiplication table

→

"Printing Precision"

```
      ⎕PP ← 4
```

A system variable to change the number of significant digits in output to 4. (Previously it was 10)

```
      (⍳10) ∘.* 1 2 .5
 1         1      1
 2         4      1.414
 3         9      1.732
 4        16      2
 5        25      2.236
 6        36      2.449
 7        49      2.646
 8        64      2.828
 9        81      3
10       100      3.162
```

The integers from 1 to 10, their squares and square roots in a table.

```
      ⎕PP ← 10
```

Changing the printing precision back to 10

Challenge:

```
      ⎕ ← VEGETABLE ← 'PEARS' ∘.≠ 'APPLES'
1 0 0 1 1 1
1 1 1 1 0 1
0 1 1 1 1 1
1 1 1 1 1 1
1 1 1 1 1 0
```

```
      (∨/~VEGETABLE) / 'PEARS'
```

→

INNER PRODUCT f.g

Inner product is an operation which reduces arrays by applying two dyadic functions.

```
      10 4 +.× 3 2
38
```

The notation is:

(array) f.g (array)

where f and g are dyadic functions which extend to arrays.

```
      +/10 4 × 3 2
```

For vectors, inner product is the same as the first function reduced over the result of the second function

```
      V ← 10 4 5
      M ← 3 2 ρ 3 6 5 1 2
      
      V +.× M
60 84
```

For a vector and a matrix, inner product is the first f reduced over the result of the second g applied to the vector and each column of the matrix

+. ×	3 5 2	6 1 4
10 4 5	60	84

60: (10×3)+(4×5)+(5×2)

84: (10×6)+(4×1)+(5×4)

```
      (+/V × M[;1]), +/V × M[;2]
```

Other dyadic functions used in inner product:

```
      V ×.- M
¯21 12
```

```
      V ⌊.+ M
7 5
```

Minimum sums

```
      V +.⌈ M
```

Sums of maximums

For a matrix and a vector, inner product is the first function reduced over the results of <u>each row</u> of the matrix applied with the second function to the vector.

```
      (3 3 ρ 1 0) ∨.∧ 0 0 1
 1 0 1
```

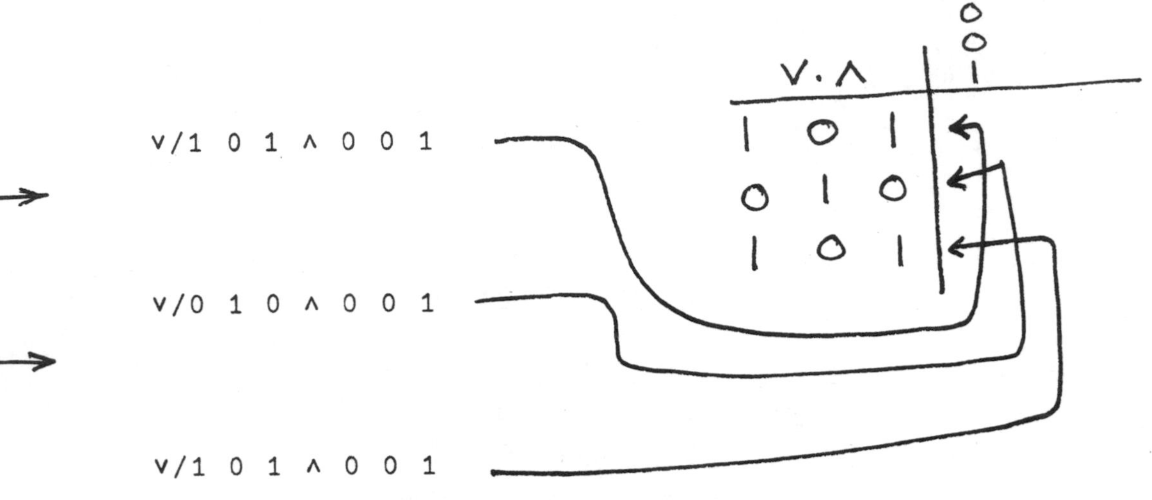

```
      ⎕ ← M ← 3 4 ⍴ ⍳12
1  2  3  4
5  6  7  8
9 10 11 12
```

For two matrices, inner product is the first function reduced over the results of <u>each row</u> of the left matrix applied with the second function to <u>each column</u> of the right matrix.

(This is the conventional "matrix product" in linear algebra)

```
      ⎕ ← N ← 4 5 ⍴ ⍳20
 1  2  3  4  5
 6  7  8  9 10
11 12 13 14 15
16 17 18 19 20
```

```
      ⎕ ← R ← M +.× N
110 120 130 140 150
246 272 298 324 350
382 424 466 508 550
```

A 3 by 4 matrix inner product with a 4 by 5 matrix

```
      ⍴R
3 5
```

The result is a 3 by 5 matrix

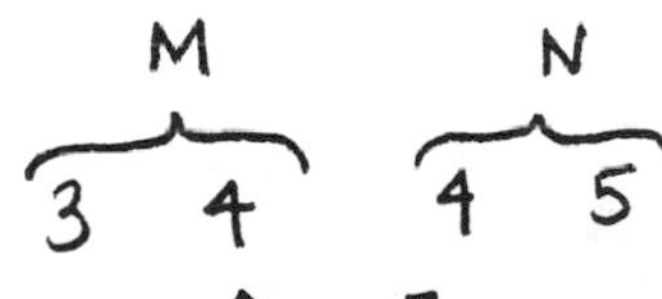


```
      (¯1↓⍴M) , 1↓⍴N
→
```

the two matrices must be "conformable" here

```
      +/M[1;] × N[;1]
→
```

The first element of the result (1st row, 1st column)

```
      R[2;3] = +/M[2;] × N[;3]
→
```

Another element of the result (second row, third column)

```
      R[;5]=(+/M[1;]×N[;5]),(+/M[2;]×N[;5]),+/M[3;]×N[;5]
1 1 1
```

The fifth column of the result

```
⎕ ← P ← 2 3 ⍴ 6 1 2 3 0 5
```

→

```
⎕ ← M ← 3 4 ⍴ ⍳12
```

→

```
⎕ ← Q ← P +.× M
```

Try this inner product

→

```
⍴Q
```

What is its size?

→

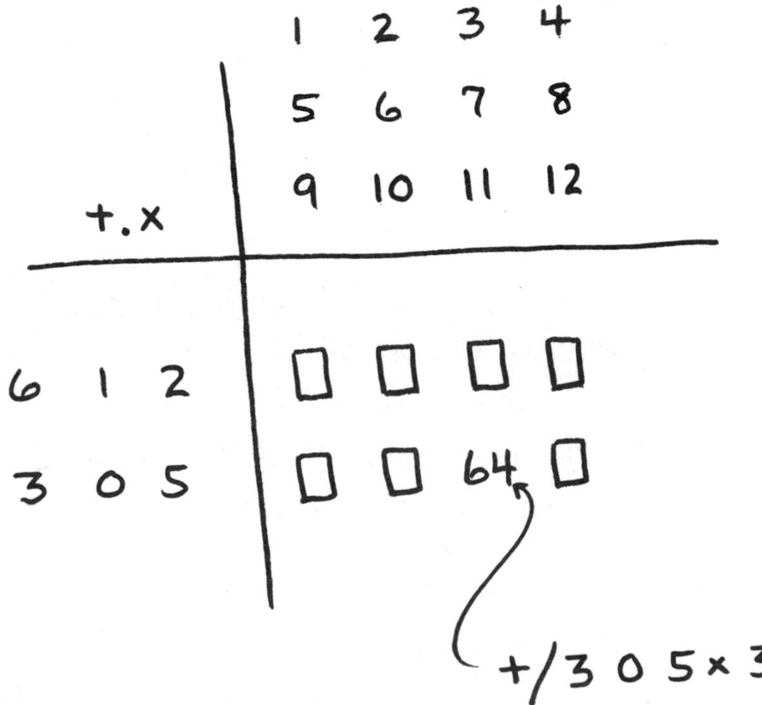

You can get Q by filling in the rest of this table.

(Q[2;3] is already done.)

```
    ⎕ ← R ← (2 3 4 ρ ι24) +.⌊ 4 2 3 ρ ι24

10   10   10
10   10   10

22   23   24
25   26   26

31   33   35
37   38   39


37   40   43
45   47   49

40   44   47
50   53   56

40   44   48
52   56   60
```

Inner product demonstrated with 3-arrays

```
    ρR

3 2 3
```

The size of the resut

```
    ρρR
```

4-dimensional

```
□ ← M ← 3 4 ρ ⍳12
```

→

Catenating a single element to a matrix:
(Along the last dimension, the element extends into a new column)

```
M , 0

1  2  3  4  0
5  6  7  8  0
9 10 11 12  0
```

Catenate 0 onto the front of M

```
0 , M
```

→

overstrike , and −

Catenating a single element to a matrix:
(Along the first dimension, the elements extends into a new row)

```
M ⍪ 0

1  2  3  4
5  6  7  8
9 10 11 12
0  0  0  0
```

Catenate 0 onto the top of M

```
0 ⍪ M
```

→

```
      M , ¯1 ¯2 ¯3
→
```

Where are these three elements catenated?

```
      M ⍪ ¯1 ¯2 ¯3 ¯4
  1  2  3  4
  5  6  7  8
  9 10 11 12
 ¯1 ¯2 ¯3 ¯4
```

These four elements are catenated as a new row (the 1st dimension)

```
      M , M
1  2  3  4  1  2  3  4
5  6  7  8  5  6  7  8
9 10 11 12  9 10 11 12
```

Matrix M catenated to matrix M

(Note that they are conformable.)

```
      ⍴ M , M
3 8
```

The resulting new size

```
      M ⍪ M
→
```

Catenate M to M along the 1st dimension

```
      ⍴ M ⍪ M
6 4
```

New rows.

```
      M ,[.5] M

 1  2  3  4
 5  6  7  8
 9 10 11 12

 1  2  3  4
 5  6  7  8
 9 10 11 12
```

The same symbol as for catenation is used , but with a fractional subscript.

Lamination creates a new dimension in the result by "stacking" arrays.

(The arrays must be conformable)

```
      ρ M ,[.5] M
2 3 4
```

[.5] means create a new dimension before the 1st dimension

```
      M ,[2.5] M
 1  1
 2  2
 3  3
 4  4

 5  5
 6  6
 7  7
 8  8

 9  9
10 10
11 11
12 12
```

[2.5] means create a new dimension after the 2nd dimension

```
      ρ M ,[2.5] M
3 4 2
```

The size of the new array

```
      V ← 2 3 5 7
      V ,[.5] V
→

      ρ V ,[.5] V
→
```

Laminating two vectors horizontally

```
      V ,[1.5] V
→
      ρ V ,[1.5] V
→
```

Laminating vertically

A REVIEW OF CATENATION AND LAMINATION

```
      ⎕ ← L ← 4 3ρ 'ABCDEFGHIJKL'
→

      L , '*'
→

      '*' ⍪ L
→

      '*' ⍪ ('*', L , '*') ⍪ '*'
*****
*ABC*
*DEF*
*GHI*
*JKL*
*****

      L ,[1] L
→

      L ,[2] L
→

      L ,[.5] L
→

      L ,[1.5] L
→

      L ,[2.5] L
→
```

```
      C ← 3 3 ρ 2 ¯1 5 1 2 1 4 0 ¯1
```

The ⌹ symbol is formed by overstriking ÷ and ⎕

⌹C produces the "inverse" of C

```
      ⌹C

 ¯0.04081632653   0.02040816327   ¯0.2244897959
 ¯0.1020408163    0.4489795918    ¯0.0612244898
  0.1632653061    0.08163265306   ¯0.1020408163
```

```
      C +.× ⌹C

1 0 0
0 1 0
0 0 1
```

The inner product of C and the inverse of C is an identity matrix.

```
      (⌹C) +.× C

1 0 0
0 1 0
0 0 1
```

SOLVING SIMULTANEOUS LINEAR EQUATIONS

```
      ⎕ ← C ← 3 3 ρ 2 ¯1 5 1 2 1 4 0 ¯1
```

→ If a matrix (C) represents the coefficients of a set of linear equations:

$$2x_1 - x_2 + 5x_3 = 13$$
$$x_1 + 2x_2 + x_3 = 0$$
$$4x_1 - x_3 = 11$$

```
      ⎕ ← B ← 13 0 11
```

→ and a vector (B) represents the constants,

```
      (⌹C) +.× B
3 ¯2 1
```

the solution set is found by the matrix (inner) product of the inverse of the coefficients matrix and the constants vector.

```
      B ⌹ C
3 ¯2 1
```

Dyadic use of ⌹ (the "matrix division" function) yields the solutions directly.

$$x_1 = 3$$
$$x_2 = {}^{-}2$$
$$x_3 = 1$$

REVIEW

Several primitive APL functions are especially designed for *array operations*. For instance, the reversal ⌽ (monadic) and rotation ⌽ (dyadic) functions rotate elements of an array. The transpose ⍉ (monadic and dyadic) function interchanges specified dimensions of an array and provides a convenient expression for array diagonals.

Two special operators—"outer product" and "inner product"—are particularly powerful. Outer product provides an alternate way to create arrays by performing a specified dyadic function on every pair of elements drawn from the arrays on the left and right. Inner product reduces two arrays by applying two dyadic functions—the first function reduced over the result of the second. (+ . × is the conventional "matrix product.") Both outer product and inner product are generalized to accept any dyadic functions which extend to arrays.

The catenation function—previously used with vectors and scalars—also applies to arrays. New rows or columns may be appended, depending on the dimension indicated in brackets [ ]. The , symbol may also be used to laminate arrays, stacking them along a specified dimension.

Finally, an overstrike symbol ⌹ is the matrix inverse/matrix divide function. It can only be used with matrices—to find their inverses (monadically) or to solve linear equation systems and least squares regressions (dyadically).

U-Program 9

MISCELLANEOUS

Contents

Identity Function +

```
      +4
4
```

```
      ⎕ ← V ← + 2 ¯2 3.7 0 ¯12 13
2 ¯2 3.7 0 ¯12 13
```

The result is identical to the numbers on the right

```
      +5
→
```

same as 0+5

Negation Function −

```
      -5
¯5
```

```
      ⎕ ← W ← - 2 ¯2 3.7 0 ¯12 13
¯2 2 ¯3.7 0 12 ¯13
```

The result is the negation of the numbers on the right

```
      -6
→
```

same as 0-6

```
      V + W
→
```

SIGNUM FUNCTION ×

```
      ×7
 1
```

The result indicates the sign of the number(s) on the right:

```
      0 < 7
 1

      ×¯5
¯1
```

1 for a positive number

0 for zero

-1 for a negative number

```
      - 0 > ¯5
→

      B ← 3 ¯4.2 0 5.8 0 ¯9
      ×B
 1 ¯1 0 1 0 ¯1

      ∇R ← SIGNUM B
[1]      R ← (0 < B) - 0 > B
      ∇
```

This expresses the signum function for any number(s) B

```
      SIGNUM B
→

      B × SIGNUM B
→

      B××B
 3 4.2 0 5.8 0 9
```

Absolute values.

RECIPROCAL FUNCTION ÷

The result is the reciprocal of the number(s) on the right.

```
      ÷2
0.5
```

```
      ÷3
```

→ same as 1÷3

```
      ÷4 5 .125 7
0.25 0.2 8 0.1428571429
```

```
      ÷10
```

→

```
      ÷100
0.01
```

EXPONENTIAL FUNCTION *

```
      *1
2.718281828
```

The result is e (the natural logarithm base) raised to the power on the right.

e (2.718281828...) raised to the power 1

```
      *2
7.389056099
```

e raised to the power 2

```
      2.718281828 * 2
7.389056096
```

e squared

```
      2.718281828 * 1
```

e (to 10 significant digits)

→

```
      POWERS ← ι8
```

Using 8 POWERS of 10 for numbers N,

```
      N ← 10 * POWERS - 1

      (1 + ÷N) * N
```

this expression converges on the value of e

```
2 2.59374246 2.704813829 2.716923932 2.718145927
      2.71828237 2.718280469 2.718281688
```

overstrike ○ and *

The Natural Logarithm (monadic ⍟)

```
      ⍟ 7.389056099 2.718281828
2 0.9999999998
```

The results are the natural logarithms of the numbers on the right.

```
      *2 1
7.389056099 2.718281828
```

2 and (1) are the powers to which you must raise e to get the numbers shown.

```
      ⍟ *3
→
```

What is the natural logarithm of e raised to the 3 power?

```
      * ⍟3
3
```

e raised to the ⍟3 power is 3

```
      B ← 10
      N ← 100
```

A base B and a number N

```
      ⍟N
4.605170186

      ⍟B
2.302585093

      (⍟N) ÷ ⍟ B
→

      (B ⍟ N) = (⍟N) ÷ ⍟ B
1

      B ⍟ N
→
```

The dyadic use of ⍟ is equivalent to dividing the natural logarithms of the Number N and the base B.

THE LOGARITHMIC FUNCTION (dyadic ⍟)

```
      10 ⍟ 100
2
```

The result is the power to which the number on the left must be raised in order to get the number on the right.

```
      10 ⍟ 10 * 2
→
```

(The number on the left is usually called the "base")

What is the logarithm of 10*2 to the base 10?

```
      10 ⍟ 1000
→
```

and the logarithm of 1000 to the base 10?

```
      10 ⍟ 10 * 3
3
```

```
      10 ⍟ 10000 100000 1000000 10
→
```

What powers of 10 are these?

```
       5 ⍟ 25
2
```

The logarithm of 25 to the base 5 is 2 (5 raised to the 2 power is 25)

```
      7 ⍟ 7 * 3
→
```

What is the logarithm of 7*3 to the base 7?

```
      3 ⍟ 81
→
```

What is the logarithm of 81 to the base 3?

```
      ( ?10) ⍟ 1
0
```

The logarithm of 1 to any positive base is 0

The Pi-times function (monadic ○)

```
      ⎕ ← PI ← ○1
3.141592654
```

The result is pi (π) times the number on the right.

```
      ○2
```

Pi times 2

→

```
      ○3 4 10 20
9.424777961 12.56637061 31.41592654 62.83185307
```

```
      ⎕PP ← 3
```

The system variable changes the number of significant digits displayed in the output.

```
      ○1
3.14
```

Now only 3 digits are printed

```
      RADII ← ⍳5

      ○RADII * 2
3.14 12.6 28.3 50.3 78.5
```

Pi times each of the RADII squared

THE TRIGONOMETRIC FUNCTIONS (dyadic ○)

The result is evaluated for the particular trigonometric function indicated on the left where 1 indicates sine
2 " cosine
3 " tangent etc.
and the number(s) on the right are expressed in radians.

```
      1 ○ ○1
¯3.43E¯15
```

The sine of π radians (180°) is close to 0.

The sine of $\frac{\pi}{4}$ radians (45°)
(to 3 significant digits)

```
      1 ○ ○÷4
.707
```

several angles: $\frac{\pi}{6}, \frac{\pi}{3}, \frac{\pi}{2}, \frac{2\pi}{3}, \frac{5\pi}{6}, \pi, \frac{7\pi}{6}, \frac{4\pi}{3}, \frac{3\pi}{2}, \frac{5\pi}{3}, \frac{11\pi}{6}, 2\pi$

```
      ⎕ ← RADIANS ← ○ ÷ 6 ÷ ⍳12
→
```

The sine of each angle

```
      1 ○ RADIANS
0.5 0.866 1 0.866 0.5 0 ¯0.5 ¯0.866 ¯1 ¯0.886 ¯0.5 0
```

The cosine of each angle

```
      2 ○ RADIANS
0.866 0.5 0 ¯0.5 ¯0.866 ¯1 ¯0.866 ¯0.5 0 0.5 0.866 1
```

The tangent of each angle

```
      3 ○ RADIANS
→
```

For any one of the angles,

```
      ANGLE ← RADIANS[? ρ RADIANS]
```

The tangent of the ANGLE equals the sine of the ANGLE divided by the cosine of the ANGLE.

```
      (3 ○ ANGLE) = (1 ○ ANGLE) ÷ 2 ○ ANGLE
1
```

It may be convenient to embody these trigonometric functions as monadic defined functions.

```
      ∇Z ← SINE ANGLE
[1]   Z ← 1 ○ ANGLE
      ∇

      ∇Z ← COSINE ANGLE
[1]   Z ← 2 ○ ANGLE
      ∇

      ∇Z ← TANGENT ANGLE
[1]   Z ← 3 ○ ANGLE
      ∇

      ∇Z ← TRIG4 ANGLE
[1]   Z ← 4 ○ ANGLE
      ∇
```

To make this family of functions complete, the following are available.

```
      (4 ○ ANGLE) = (1 + ANGLE * 2) * .5

1

      ∇Z ← TRIG0 ANGLE
[1]   Z ← 0 ○ ANGLE
      ∇

      (0 ○ ANGLE) = (1 - ANGLE * 2) * .5

1
```

The hyperbolic trigonometric functions

```
      ∇Z ← SINH ANGLE
[1]   Z ← 5 ○ ANGLE
      ∇

      ∇Z ← COSH ANGLE
[1]   Z ← 6 ○ ANGLE
      ∇

      ∇Z ← TANH ANGLE
[1]   Z ← 7 ○ ANGLE
      ∇
```

```
    ∇ANGLE ← ARCSINE X
[1]  ANGLE ← ¯1 ○ X
    ∇

    ∇ANGLE ← ARCCOSINE X
[1]  ANGLE ← ¯2 ○ X
    ∇

    ∇ANGLE ← ARCTANGENT X
[1]  ANGLE ← ¯3 ○ X
    ∇

    ∇ANGLE ← ARCTRIG4 X
[1]  ANGLE ← ¯4 ○ X
    ∇

    ∇ANGLE ← ARCSINH X
[1]  ANGLE ← ¯5 ○ X
    ∇

    ∇ANGLE ← ARCCOSH X
[1]  ANGLE ← ¯6 ○ X
    ∇

    ∇ANGLE ← ARCTANH X
[1]  ANGLE ← ¯7 ○ X
    ∇
```

The arc-trigonometric functions

where ¯4○X is
(¯1+X*2)*.5

Defined programs for converting angles in degrees to radians and vice versa.

```
      ∇RADIANS ← DEGREES ANGLE
[1]   RADIANS ←  ○ANGLE÷180
      ∇


      DEGREES 45

0.785


      SINE DEGREES 30

0.5


      DEGREES 60

→


      COSINE DEGREES 60

→


      (2 ○ 60 × ○ ÷ 180) = COSINE DEGREES 60

1

      (DEGREES 45) × 360 ÷ ○ 2

→
```

```
      ∇DEGREES ← RADIANS ANGLE

DEFN ERROR

      ∇DEGREES←RADIANS ANGLE
                          ^
```

This attempt at defining a program produces a DEFINITION ERROR because the name RADIANS has already been assigned! (see p. 171)

```
      RADIANS

0.524 1.05 1.57 2.09 2.62 3.14 3.67 4.19 4.71 5.24 5.76 6.28

      )ERASE RADIANS
```

The)ERASE system command will erase any names--including programs-- listed immediately afterward.

```
      ∇DEGREES ← RADIANS ANGLE
[1]   DEGREES ← ANGLE÷○÷180
      ∇
```

RADIANS is erased, so a new program with that name can now be defined.

```
      RADIANS ○1

180
```

Pi radians is equivalent to 180 degrees

```
      RADIANS ○÷4

→
```

$\frac{\pi}{4}$ radians = ? degrees

```
      (○÷3) = DEGREES RADIANS ○÷3

1
```

An identity

```
      30 = RADIANS DEGREES 30

→
```

Recursion is a process which in its description refers to itself -- hence causing repeated use of the same process. For example:

```
     ∇Z ← A MEMBER B
[1]  →(0 = ρB)/Z ← 0
[2]  Z ← (A = 1 ↑ B) ∨ A MEMBER 1 ↓ B∇
```

The definition of MEMBER include itself in its own definition. MEMB is a recursive program which determines whether the element(on the left are members of thos on the right. (same as dyadic ∈)

```
     4 MEMBER ι5
1
```

```
     TΔMEMBER ← ι2
```

Tracing lines 1 and 2

```
     Y ← ι2 + X ← 3
```

Assigning both X and Y values in one expression

```
     X MEMBER Y
MEMBER[1]        the first execution of MEMBER
MEMBER[1]        the second
MEMBER[1]        the third
MEMBER[1]        the fourth.
MEMBER[1]        the fifth
MEMBER[1] 0      the sixth terminates immediately on line [1]
MEMBER[2] 0      the fifth terminates (with an explicit result of 0)
MEMBER[2] 0      the fourth terminates ( "   "   "   "   " )
MEMBER[2] 1      the third terminates (with an explicit result of 1)
MEMBER[2] 1      the second terminates ( "   "   "   "   " )
MEMBER[2] 1      the first terminates ( "   "   "   "   " )
 1 ←
```

the final result--yes, X (3) is a member of Y (1 2 3 4 5)

```
     TΔMEMBER ← ι0
```

Untracing

```
     X MEMBER Y ← 2 × Y
→
```

Execute MEMBER for the same X but twice the Y.

```
     'R' MEMBER 'WORD'
→
```

MEMBER with literals

```
     'RAW' MEMBER 'WORD'
1 0 1
```

FAC is also <u>Recursive</u>. It is a program which computes the "factorial" of nonnegative integer N by repeated multiplication.

```
      ∇Z ← FAC N
[1]   Z ← 1
[2]   →(N = 0)/0
[3]   Z ← N × FAC N-1∇
```

Z (the final resultant) is the value of N times the result of the execution of FAC for N-1

```
      FAC 5
120

      FAC 4
→

      ∧/(FAC 3)=(3×FAC 2),(3×2×FAC 1),(3×2×1×FAC 0)
1

      FAC 0
→

      ×/⍳3
→

      ×/⍳4
→

      (!5) = ×/⍳5
1

      !5
→
```

5 × 4 × 3 × 2 × 1

FACTORIAL FUNCTION! (MONADIC)

```
      !5
120
```

The result is the product of the integers from 1 to the number given on the right

```
      ! 5 3 1
120 6 1
```

Factorials of 5 3 and 1

```
      !4 2
```

→

Factorials of 4 and 2 ?

```
      !12
4.79E8
```

Factorial of 12 is (approx.) 4.79×10^8

```
      !2.6
```

→

Estimate this one
(This function extends to fractions)

```
      !8
40320
```

COMBINATIONS FUNCTION! (DYADIC)

```
      1 ! 8
8
```

The result is the number of combinations which may be formed by taking the number of things on the left from the number of things on the right.

```
      2 ! 8
```

→

How many combinations can be formed from 8 things, taking 2 at a time?

```
      (3 ! 8) = (!8) ÷ (!3) × !8-3
1
```

Equivalent expressions for the combinations of 8 things, taking 3 at a time.

```
      3 ! 8
```

→

What value does this have ?

```
      8 ! 3
```

→

What meaning could this have ?

BASE VALUE FUNCTION ⊥

The result is the value of the number on the right expressed in the base of the number on the left.

Numbers in base 2 are converted into their decimal values.

```
      2 ⊥ 0
0
      2 ⊥ 1
1
      2 ⊥ 1 0
2
      2 ⊥ 1 1
3
      2 ⊥ 1 0 0
4
      2 ⊥ 1 0 1
→
      2 ⊥ 1 0 1 1 1
→
      (1 × 2*4) + (0 × 2*3) + (1 × 2*2) + (1 × 2*1) + 1 × 2*0
→
      (1 × 5*3) + (4 × 5*2) + (2 × 5*1) + 3 × 5*0
→
      5 ⊥ 1 4 2 3
238
```

The base 5 value of 1 4 2 3

```
      1339 = +/2 4 7 3 × 8 * 3 2 1 0
1
```

Base 8

```
      8 ⊥ 2 4 7 3
1339

      (8 ⊥ 2 4 7 3) - 8 ⊥ 2 4 6 3
→

      (8 ⊥ 2 4 7 3) - 8 ⊥ 2 3 7 3
→

      (8 ⊥ 2 4 7 3) - 8 ⊥ 1 1 1 1
→
```

Base 10

```
      10 ⊥ 1 7 7 6
→

      10 ⊥ 4 4 4
→

      10 10 10 ⊥ 4 4 4
444

      10 10 10 10 ⊥ 1 7 7 6
→
```

A scalar on the left extends to a vector on the right,

or matches (in size) a vector on the left.

The base value function can be used with several different bases. For example, 24 (hours/day) 60 (min./hour) 60 (sec./min.)

```
      24 60 60 ⊥ 1 3 2
3782
```

the number of seconds in 1 hour 3 minutes 2 sec.

```
      A ← 13 60 60
      B ← 1 3 2
      ⎕ ← R ← A ⊥ B
3782
```

Notice that the left-most element of A does not affect the result.

```
      W ← 3600 60 1
      ⎕ ← R ← W +.× B
→
```

Another way of looking at it -- W is a "weight" vector.

```
      A ← 7 24 60 60
      B ← 2 10 3 4
      ⎕ ← W ← (×/1↓A) , (×/2↓A) , (×/3↓A) , 1
→
```

This example shows (more generally) how W may be produced.

```
      (⎕ ←  A ⊥ B) = W +.× B
208984
1
```

The number of seconds in 2 days 10 hours 3 min. 4 sec. (208984) -- found by base value -- is identical to the inner product of W and B.

```
      1780 3 12 ⊥ 5 2 6
→
```

The number of inches in 5 yards 2 feet 6 inches (Note that 12 is inches per feet, 3 is feet per yard, and the 1780 is inconsequential)

```
      1780 3 12 ⊤ 210
5 2 6
```

Use ⊤ to convert back to yards, feet and inches.

```
      24 60 60 ⊤ 3782
→
```

Convert 3782 seconds into

__ hours __ minutes __ sec.

```
      10 10 10 ⊤ 360
3 6 0
```

The result is the representation of the number on the right in the base system on the left.

Base-10 representation of 360

```
      (4 ρ 10) ⊤ (4 ρ 10) ⊥ 2 0 0 1
→
```

What is the base-10 representation of the base-10 value of 2 0 0 1 . ?

```
      (5 ρ 2) ⊤ 23
1 0 1 1 1

      (3 ρ 2) ⊤ 23
1 1 1
```

The representation is truncated if there are not enough places made available on the left of ⊤.

```
      2 2 2 ⊤ 5
1 0 1

      2 2 2 ⊤ 4
→

      2 2 ⊤ 3
1 1

      2 2 ⊤ 2
1 0

      2 ⊤ 1
1

      2 ⊤ 0
→
```

Numbers in base 10 represented in base 2

```
      2 2 2 ⊤ 4 4 4 4 4
1 1 1 1 1
0 0 0 0 0
0 0 0 0 0
```

With a vector on the right, each element is represented in the bases on the left (and displayed as columns.)

```
      2 2 2 ⊤ 4 5 6 7 8
```

→

What are the base 2 representations of 4 5 6 7 and 8?

```
      2 2 2 ⊤ ⍳8
0 0 0 1 1 1 1 0
0 1 1 0 0 1 1 0
1 0 1 0 1 0 1 0
```

Notice that there are not enough places to represent 8 fully, so it is truncated.

```
      N ← 3
      (N⍴2) ⊤ (⍳2*N)-1
```

For N of 3,

evaluate this expression

→

```
      ⍉(N⍴2) ⊤ (⍳2*N)-1
0 0 0
0 0 1
0 1 0
0 1 1
1 0 0
1 0 1
1 1 0
1 1 1
```

Its transpose reveals a familiar pattern -- base 2 representations of successive integers -- found in the rows.

TRUTH is a program which produces a table of <u>all</u> the logical (base 2) combinations of order N.

```
      ∇TABLE ← TRUTH N
[1]   TABLE ← ⍉ (Nρ2) ⊤ (⍳2*N)-1
      ∇
```

```
      TRUTH 2
```

→

Display the TRUTH table of order 2

```
      TRUTH 3
0 0 0
0 0 1
0 1 0
0 1 1
1 0 0
1 0 1
1 1 0
1 1 1
```

The TRUTH table of order 3

```
      ρTRUTH 4
```

→

What is the size of the TRUTH table of order 4 ?

```
     ∇VALUE ← BASES  DECODE  VECTOR
[1]  VALUE ← 1↑VECTOR
[2]  →(0=ρBASES←1↓BASES)/0
[3]  VALUE ← (VALUE××/BASES) + BASES DECODE 1↓VECTOR
     ∇
```

DECODE is a recursive definition of the base-value function (⊥).

Note: ∇DECODE[.5]BASES←(ρVECTOR)ρBASES∇ will permit scalar BASES.

```
     1780 3 12  DECODE  5 2 6
```

→

How many inches in 5 yards, 2 feet, 6 inches?

```
     ∇VECTOR ← BASES  ENCODE  VALUE
[1]  VECTOR ← BASES|VALUE
[2]  →(0=ρBASES←1↓BASES)/0
[3]  VECTOR ← (⌊VALUE÷×/BASES) , BASES ENCODE (×/BASES)|VALUE
     ∇
```

ENCODE is a recursive definition of the representation function (⊤).

Note: scalar VALUE only

```
     1780 3 12  ENCODE  210
```

→

How many yards, feet, inches in 210 inches?

EXECUTE FUNCTION ⍎

```
      3+4
7
      '3+4'
3+4
      ⍎'3+4'
7
      ⍎'A←3+4'
      A
7
      ⍎(A>10)/'D←4×5'
      D
```

Normal execution of a numeric expression

" " a literal "

Converting a literal to a numeric

⍎ strips off the quote marks and executes the expression inside

⍎ can be used to assign variables or execute programs under certain conditions

→

FORMAT FUNCTION ⍕

```
      ⍕⍳5
1 2 3 4 5
      ⍴⍕⍳5
9
      '1 2 3 4 5' = ⍕⍳5
      ⍎⍕⍳5
1 2 3 4 5
      ⍕⍎'⍳5'
1 2 3 4 5
      (⍴⍎⍕⍳5) = ⍴⍕⍎'⍳5'
```

Converting a numeric to a literal

(spaces included)

⍕ has the effect of putting quote marks around the value of the expression and representing it in the simplest literal format.

→

⍕ and ⍎ are (kind of) inverses

→

DYADIC FORMAT ⍕

⍕ has a dyadic usage: to represent values (as literals) in a specified format.

```
      1 ⍕ ⍳5
1.0 2.0 3.0 4.0 5.0
```

1 place after the decimal point

```
      2 ⍕ ⍳5
```

→ Display 2 places after the decimal point

General Formatting

More generally, ⍕ can be used with a vector left argument:

V[1] is the number of spaces in the horizontal field for each element of A

V[2] indicates how many places after the decimal point (+) or use of E-notation (−).

```
      V ← 10 2
      A ← (⍳10) ∘.* 1  2  .5
      V ⍕ A
      1.00        1.00        1.00
      2.00        4.00        1.41
      3.00        9.00        1.73
      4.00       16.00        2.00
      5.00       25.00        2.24
      6.00       36.00        2.45
      7.00       49.00        2.65
      8.00       64.00        2.83
      9.00       81.00        3.00
     10.00      100.00        3.16
```

The integers from 1 to 10, their squares + square roots formatted in a table with 10 columns each and 2 places after the decimal point for each number.

```
      ⍴V⍕A
```

→

[Compare with table on p. 150]

```
      +/⍳10
55

      +\⍳10
1 3 6 10 15 21 28 36 45 55

 (+/⍳1),(+/⍳2),(+/⍳3),(+/⍳4),(+/⍳5),(+/⍳6),(+/⍳7),(+/⍳8),(+/⍳9),+/⍳10

      (×\⍳10) = !⍳10
1 1 1 1 1 1 1 1 1 1

      |\⍳10

      ∨\0 0 1 0 1 1 0

      ∧\1 1 0 1 0 0 1

      ∇VALUE ← BASES DECODE ARRAY
[1]   VALUE ← ARRAY +.× ⌽×\⌽1↓BASES,1
      ∇
```

Sum reduction

Sum scan gives all the cumulative sums.

→

\ may be used with any dyadic scalar function

→

→

→

An alternative definition for DECODE (⊥) using scan \

(This program generalizes to ARRAYs.)

EXPANSION FUNCTION \

The result is an array expanded to the size of the numbers on the left (always 0s and 1s) with spaces (for literals) or 0s (for numericals) inserted in the array on the right.

```
      1 0 1 0 1 / 'ABCDE'
ACE
```

Expansion \ and compression / are related

```
      1 0 1 0 1 \ 'ACE'
A C E
```

Spaces are inserted in the literal result.

```
      ⎕ ← R ← (Q ← 1 0 1 0 1 1 0 0) / V ← 2 3 5 7 11 13 17 19
2 5 11 13
```

A numerical vector is compressed.

```
      Q \ R
2 0 5 0 11 13 0 0
```

A numerical vector is expanded: elements of R corresponding to 1s in Q are preserved, 0s replace the others.

```
      ρR
→
```

What is the size of R?

```
      +/Q
→
```

How many 1s in Q?

```
      (ρQ) = ρQ\R
→
```

The size of Q and Q\R compared.

```
      L ← 1 1 1 1 0 1 1 1 1 1 0 0 1 1 0 0 1 1 1 1 1 1
      L \ 'BACKSLASHOREXPAND'
→
```

Preserve the elements of the right where there are 1s in L; spaces replace the elements where there are 0s.

```
      U ← 1 0 1 1 0

      U \ 3 3 ρ ι9

1 0 2 3 0
4 0 5 6 0
7 0 8 9 0
```

Expansion with matrices

Expanding the last dimension (columns)

```
      U ⍀ 3 3 ρ ι9

1 2 3
0 0 0
4 5 6
7 8 9
0 0 0
```

Expanding the first dimension (rows)

```
      (12 ρ 1 0 0) \'APL\' ; (3 ρ 10) ⊤ 212 × 30

→
```

An expression of tribute to a certain computer system . . .

REVIEW

Numerous functions are available in APL for special purposes: monadic use of + - × ÷ , the logarithm ⍟ function (monadic and dyadic), pi-times ○ (monadic), all the circular functions ○ (dyadic)—including sine, cosine, and tangent—factorial and combinations ! , base value ⊥ and representation ⊤ , execute ⍎ , format ⍕ , scan \ , and expansion \ .

Recursive programs may be defined in APL by including a program name within its own program definition. Such a program will execute itself in the process of executing itself, etc. Recursion is an extremely powerful programming technique . . . and a powerful concept!

APL Bogglers

Contents

A collection of APL expressions which boggle the mind. Some are special cases; some are implementation anomalies; and some are open mathematical questions—but all are syntactically allowable APL expressions which have results you can try to predict.

```
0 ÷ 0

0 * 0

1 ⍟ 1

0 ! 0

0 + ⍳0

(⍳0) = ⍳0

(⍳0) ⍴ 1

1 ↑ ⍳0

6 ↑ ⍳5

6 ↓ ⍳5
```

```
!1.5

⍋8 8 8 8 9

⌽⍳5

0 1 ⊤ 98.6

10 10 10 ⊤ ¯34

¯2 ⊥ ¯1 1 0 1

¯2 ¯2 ¯2 ¯2 ¯2 ⊤ 13
```

```
+/⍳0

-/⍳0

×/⍳0

÷/⍳0

=/⍳0

</⍳0

≤/⍳0

≥/⍳0

>/⍳0

≠/⍳0
```

```
⌈/⍳0

⌊/⍳0

|/⍳0

∧/⍳0

∨/⍳0

*/⍳0

⍟/⍳0

!/⍳0
```

```
''''

ρ'CAN''T'

=\'AAA'

÷\0 0 0 0 0

0\⍳0

0\''
```

```
ρ5+,4

ρ(1ρ4)+1 1ρ3

ρ7ρ''

+/[1]3 0 4ρ2

+/[2]3 0 4ρ2

+/[3]3 0 4ρ2
```

```
A ← 10ρ5

A[10ρ1] ← ι10

A


V ← 2 3 5 7

V[ ]

V[ι0]


V[ ]←9

V


V[ι0]←9

V


V[3]←ι0

V
```

```
M ← 3 4 ρ ι12

ρM[1;]

ρM[;?]

ρM[1 3;2 4]←1+M[1 3;2 4]←9


1 0 ↑ M

1 0 ↓ M

0 0 ↑ M

0 0 ↓ M

4 5 ↑ M

4 5 ↓ M


2 2 ⍉ M
```

```
      S ← 5

      (S←8) × S



      T ← 8.8

      (T←5) × ⌈T



      ∇Z←F  X
[1]   Z←X+Y
      ∇


      ∇Z←G  Y
[1]   Z←F  Y
      ∇


      Y←3
      G  4
```

Summary of APL*

Contents

**Note*: These summaries cover the material presented in this book but are incomplete in some places (marked *). For complete details consult a reference manual such as APL/360 Reference Manual, 2nd edit., by Sandra Pakin, S.R.A., 1972; or APLUM Reference Manual, 2nd edit., by Clark Wiedmann, University of Massachusetts, 1977.

SUMMARY OF DYADIC SCALAR FUNCTIONS

"Dyadic scalar functions" are those dyadic APL primitive functions that extend the way they perform on scalars to higher order arrays.

SYMBOL	NAME	DEFINITION	EXAMPLE
+	Plus	Standard Arithmetic	(3+4)=7
-	Minus		(8-3)=5
×	Times		(2×3)=6
÷	Divide		(10÷5)=2
=	Equals	Result is 1 if the relation is true; result is 0 if the relation is false.	(4=4)=1
<	Less-Than		(4<5)=1
≤	Not Greater		(4≤3)=0
≥	Not Less		(4≥3)=1
>	Greater-Than		(4>5)=0
≠	Not Equal		(4≠4)=0
⌈	Maximum	Result is the larger	(5⌈8)=8
⌊	Minimum	Result is the smaller	(5⌊8)=5
∣	Residue	Result is remainder (A∣B)=B-A×⌊B÷A+A=0	(5∣8)=3
∧	And	(0 0 1 1∧0 1 0 1) = 0 0 0 1	
∨	Or	(0 0 1 1∨0 1 0 1) = 0 1 1 1	
⍲	Nand	(0 0 1 1⍲0 1 0 1) = 1 1 1 0	
⍱	Nor	(0 0 1 1⍱0 1 0 1) = 1 0 0 0	
*	Power	Exponentiation	(3*2)=9
⍟	Logarithm	(Base) log (Number)	(3⍟9)=2
!	Combinations	(R!N)=(!N)÷(!R)×!N-R	(3!8)=56

SYMBOL	NAME	DEFINITION	EXAMPLE
○	Circular	1○(radians) is Sine	(1○○1)=0
		2○(radians) is Cosine	(2○○1)=1
		3○(radians) is Tangent	(3○○÷4)=1
		4○(radians is (1+(radians)*2)*.5	
		5○(radians) is Hyperbolic Sine	
		6○(radians) is Hyperbolic Cosine	
		7○(radians) is Hyperbolic Tangent	
		-7○(number) is Arc Hyperbolic Tangent	
		-6○(number) is Arc Hyperbolic Cosine	
		-5○(number) is Arc Hyperbolic Sine	
		-4○(number) is (-1+(number)*2)*.5	
		-3○(number) is Arc Tangent	(¯3○1)=○÷4
		-2○(number) is Arc Cosine	(¯2○1)=1
		-1○(number) is Arc Sine	(¯1○0)=1
		0○(number) is (1-(number)*2)*.5	

SUMMARY OF MONADIC SCALAR FUNCTIONS

"Monadic scalar functions" are those monadic APL primitive functions that extend the way they perform on scalars to higher order arrays.

<table>
<tr><th>SYMBOL</th><th>NAME</th><th>DEFINITION</th><th>EXAMPLE</th></tr>
<tr><td>+</td><td>Identity</td><td>(+(number))=(number)</td><td>(+4)=4</td></tr>
<tr><td>-</td><td>Negation</td><td>(-(number))=0-(number)</td><td>(-4)=¯4</td></tr>
<tr><td>×</td><td>Signum</td><td>(×(number))=
((number)>0)-(number)<0</td><td>(×¯4)=¯1</td></tr>
<tr><td>÷</td><td>Reciprocal</td><td>(÷(number))=1÷(number)</td><td>(÷4)=.25</td></tr>
<tr><td>~</td><td>Not</td><td>(~(number))=1-(number)</td><td>(~0 1)=1 0</td></tr>
<tr><td>|</td><td>Absolute Value</td><td>(number)⌈-(number)</td><td>(|¯8)=8</td></tr>
<tr><td>⌊</td><td>Floor</td><td>(number)-1|(number)</td><td>(⌊3.4)=3</td></tr>
<tr><td>⌈</td><td>Ceiling</td><td>(number)+1|-(number)</td><td>(⌈3.4)=4</td></tr>
<tr><td>?</td><td>Random</td><td>A random choice from
⍳(number)</td><td>(?10)=7</td></tr>
<tr><td>*</td><td>Exponential</td><td>(2.71828...)*(number)</td><td>(*1)=2.71828</td></tr>
<tr><td>*</td><td>Natural Logarithm</td><td>(2.71828...)⍟(number)</td><td>(⍟2.71828)=1</td></tr>
<tr><td>○</td><td>Pi-times</td><td>(3.14159...)×(number)</td><td>(○1)=3.14159</td></tr>
<tr><td>!</td><td>Factorial</td><td>×/⍳(number)</td><td>(!3)=6</td></tr>
</table>

SUMMARY OF MIXED FUNCTIONS

"Mixed functions" are those APL primitive functions which have certain requirements for the arrays they use as arguments (and, hence, do not extend the way they perform on scalars to higher order arrays).

SYMBOL	NAME	DEFINITION/SYNTAX	EXAMPLE
,	Catenation	Chaining: (array),(array)	'AB','CDE' ABCDE
⍳	Iota	Index generator: ⍳(scalar)	⍳4 1 2 3 4
[ ]	Indexing	Selection of specified elements: vector [array] matrix [array;array] array[array;...;array]	2 3 5 7[3] 5 (2 3⍴⍳6)[2;2] 5 (2 3 4⍴⍳24)[2;3;] 21 22 23 24
⍴	Rho	Size of array: ⍴ (array)	⍴2 3 5 7 4
/	Compression	Selection of specified elements: (logical vector)/(array)	0 1 1 0/2 3 5 7 3 5
∊	Membership	Result is 1 if element(s) on left are found on right; otherwise 0: (array)∊(array)	3∊2 3 5 7 1
↑	Take	Take first (+) or last (-) elements: (vector)↑(array)	3↑2 3 5 7 2 3 5
↓	Drop	Drop first (+) or last (-) elements: (vector)↓(array)	3↓2 3 5 7 7
?	Deal	(scalar) unique random integers from ⍳(scalar): (scalar) ? (scalar)	5?5 3 1 5 2 4

-- Continued --

SYMBOL	NAME	DEFINITION/SYNTAX	EXAMPLE
⍋	Grade-up	Result is the permutation integers which order a vector -ascending: ⍋(vector) -descending: ⍒(vector)	⍋30 20 40 10 4 2 1 3
⍒	Grade-down		⍒30 20 40 10 3 1 2 4
⍳	Index-of	Result is least indices of (array) in (vector) (vector) ⍳ (array)	*'ABCDE'*⍳*'AX'* 1 6
⍴	Restructure	Puts (array) in new structure (vector) ⍴ (array)	2 3⍴⍳6 1 2 3 4 5 6
,	Ravel	Strings out (array) into a vector ,(array)	,2 3⍴⍳6 1 2 3 4 5 6
⌽	Reversal	Reverses elements of an (array) about axis I ⌽[I] (array)	⌽[2]2 3⍴⍳6 3 2 1 6 5 4
⌽	Rotate	Revolves specified numbers of elements of an (array) (array) ⌽[I] (array)	1 ¯1⌽[2]2 3⍴⍳6 2 3 1 6 4 5
⍉	Transpose	Reverses order of axes ⍉(array)	⍉2 3⍴⍳6 1 4 2 5 3 6
⍉	Dyadic Transpose	Axis I of (array) becomes axis (vector)[I] of result (vector) ⍉ (array)	1 1⍉2 3⍴⍳6 1 5
⌹	Matrix Inverse	Result is inverse of matrix ⌹(matrix)	*M*+.×⌹*M*←2 2⍴10 1 0 0 1
⌹	Matrix Divide	Result is (⌹(matrix B))+.×(matrix A) (matrix A) ⌹ (matrix B)	Solution to simultaneous linear equations with coefficients B and constants A

-- Continued --

SYMBOL	NAME	DEFINITION/SNYTAX	EXAMPLE
⊥	Base-value	Decoding base-10 value of right (array) in base system of left (array) (array) ⊥ (array)	24 60 60⊥1 2 3 3723
⊤	Representation	Encoding right (array) in base system of left (array) (array) ⊤(array)	24 60 60⊤3723 1 2 3
⍎	Execute	Removes quote marks and evaluates (vector) ⍎ (vector)	⍎'3+4' 7
⍕	Format	Displays (array) as a literal ⍕(array)	⍕⍳5 1 2 3 4 5
⍕	Dyadic Format	Displays (array) as a literal with (vector)[1] column spacing and (vector) [2] significant digits. (vector)⍕ (array)	6 1⍕2 3 4 2.0 3.0 4.0
\	Expansion	Expansion of (array) by (logical vector) logical (vector)\ (array)	1 0 1 0 1\'*APL*' *A P L*

SUMMARY OF OPERATORS

An APL "operator" requires a function or functions (given as argument(s)) to apply to arrays. The functions must be scalar dyadic functions.

SYMBOL	NAME	DEFINITION/SYNTAX	EXAMPLE
/	Reduction	The result is obtained by inserting the (dyadic function) between the elements of the (array) along a specified axis I (function)/[I] (array)	+/[1]2 3⍴⍳6 5 7 9
∘.	Outer Product	The result is an array obtained by applying the (dyadic function) to every pair of elements in the (arrays) given (array)∘. (function)(array)	(⍳5)∘.⍳5 1 2 3 4 5 2 4 6 8 10 3 6 9 12 15 4 8 12 16 20 5 10 15 20 25
	Inner Product	The result is an array obtained by reducing (/) the left (dyadic function) over the result of the right (dyadic function) applied to rows of the left (array) and columns of the right (array) (array)(function) . (function)(array)	(3 2⍴⍳6)+.×2 3⍴⍳6 9 12 15 19 26 33 29 40 59
\	Scan	The result is an array of the same size as the given (array) where each element is obtained by reducing (/) the elements up to and including it along a specified axis [I] (function)\[I](array)	+\[2]2 3⍴⍳6 1 3 6 4 9 15

SUMMARY OF COMMANDS

An APL command causes the computer to carry out some action which has an effect on programming activity.

SYMBOL	NAME	DEFINITION/SYNTAX	EXAMPLE
←	Assignment	Gives a name to some data. (name) ← (data)	*SERIES*←9000 or *NAME*←'*HAL*'
→	Branch	Changes order of execution of statements in a program. → (line number) or → (line label)	→(*COUNTER*)/7 or →4×⍳*A*=0 or →*END*
∆	Trace	The result of each (line number) in (program name) is displayed as the program is executed. *T* program name ∆ ← (line numbers)	*T*∆*SOLVE*←1 4 5 6
∆	Stop	The (program) automatically halts at each (line number). *S* program name ∆←(line numbers)	*S*∆*SOLVE*←3 12
⎕	Quad	For input: ⎕ in an expression For output: ⎕ ← (expression)	*N*←⎕ ⎕: 7 ⎕←*N* 7
⍞	Quote-Quad	For literal input: ⍞ in an expression For output (without a carriage return): ⍞ ← (expression)	*L*←⍞ *WORDS* ⍞←*L* *WORDS* ↑ (position of type ball)

SUMMARY OF PROGRAM DEFINITION SYNTAX

The syntax of an APL program determines how it may be used. Syntax may be dyadic (2 arguments), monadic (1 argument), or nyladic (0 arguments) and may have an explicit result or no explicit result. Examples of these six different syntaxes are shown in the program definitions below:

	WITH EXPLICIT RESULT	NO EXPLICIT RESULT
DYADIC	∇*VALUE*←*X POLY C* [1] *VALUE*←+/*X*×*C*⋆⍳ρ*C* ∇	∇*H BASEBALL AB* [1] '*YOUR BATTING AVERAGE*' [2] *H*÷*AB* ∇
MONADIC	∇*X*←*AVERAGE X* [1] *X*←(+/*X*)÷ρ*X* ∇	∇*AREA S* [1] '*AREA OF SQUARE S IS*' [2] *S*⋆2 ∇
NYLADIC	∇*VALUE*←*PI* [1] *VALUE*←○1 ∇	∇*ROLL* [1] '*THE DICE ARE*' [2] ?6 6 ∇

SUMMARY OF FUNDAMENTAL PROGRAMMING CONCEPTS

CONCEPT	EXPLANATION	EXAMPLE
Data	Constants: numerical values or literal values.	3.10 '*ABC*'
Function	A specific computational operation: "monadic" (one argument) or "dyadic" (two arguments) or both.	÷8 3+4
Variable	An entity, with a name, containing data which may be changed.	*N*
Command	An explicit order which causes the computer to take some action.	*N*←5
Expression	A combination of data and function(s) or command(s) or program(s).	3×4+5
Evaluation	Giving the value resulting from substituting values for variables, executing programs, and performing functions (rightmost first) in an expression.	3×4+5 27
Error Report	Brief diagnostic information about the type and location of the cause for failure of an expression to be evaluated.	2 4×1 3 5 *LENGTH ERROR*
Array	Rectangular-structured data: scalar, vector, matrix, 3-array, 4-array, etc.	2 4 6
Parallel Processing	Use of functions on arrays in an element-by-element fashion.	2 4 6×1 3 5
Program	An ordered sequence of expressions.	
Definition	"Writing" a program. (Entering a program in the computer.)	∇*Z*←*MEAN X* [1] *Z*←(+/*X*)÷ρ*X*∇
Execution	"Running" a program. (The computer evaluating expressions in a program, line-by-line.)	*MEAN* 70 75 95
Result	The "answer". (The consequences of executing a program.)	80
Sub-program	Programs which are used in expressions within other programs.	∇*Z*←*VARIANCE X* [1] *Z*←*MEAN*(*X*-*MEAN X*)⋆2∇

-- Continued --

CONCEPT	EXPLANATION	EXAMPLE
Recursion	A program using its own name in its definition. (A program executing itself repeatedly.)	∇*SUM*←*GAUSS N* [1] *SUM*←0 [2] →(*N*=0)/0 [3] *SUM*←*N*+*GAUSS N*-1 ∇
Iteration	A program executing certain expressions repeatedly--in a "loop."	∇*TRIANGULAR N;I* [1] *I*←0 [2] *I*←*I*+1 [3] *PRINT*: +/⍳*I* [4] →(*I*<*N*)/2 ∇
Names	Identification of programs and variables (**beginning** with an alphabetic letter):	
Local	- variable names within a program **only**	*N* and *I* and *PRINT* in *TRIANGULAR* above
Global	- variable names within the entire active workspace	*N*←5
Workspace	The working area in the computer available for (disk) storage of programs and variables.	)*CLEAR* *CLEAR WS*
Suspension	The condition of a program after encountering an error in one of its expressions: partially completed, "suspended" on a particular line.	*TRIANGULAR* '*NUMBER*' 1 *SYNTAX ERROR* *TRIANGULAR*[4] →(*I*<*N*)/2 ∧
Debugging	Any methods of pinpointing errors ("bugs") in programs and fixing them.	from above *N*←5 →4
Interactive Program	A program which interacts with the user, i.e. typically prints output, accepts input, alternatingly.	*DRILL* *WHAT IS* 3×4 ? ⎕: 12 *WHAT IS* 9×7 ? ⎕: 63 etc.
Input	-Data entered in the computer	
Output	-Data displayed by the computer	
Simulation	A program which simulates some real-world phenomenon via a mathematical/computational model--usually a simplification and possibly a distortion.	∇*TEMPER THRESHOLD* [1] *EMOTION*←0 [2] *NEW*: *EVENT*←?10 [3] *EMOTION*←*EVENT* + *EMOTION*÷2 [4] →(*EMOTION*>*THRESHOLD*)/*MAD* [5] →*NEW* [6] *MAD*: '**!?!*!' [7] →1 ∇

SUMMARY OF ERROR REPORTS

Error reports give general diagnostic information about the type and location of errors in expressions.

TYPE	INTERPRETATION	EXAMPLE
SYNTAX	Faulty syntax in an expression, i.e. a function or program used without value(s) in the proper place	4+3× *SYNTAX ERROR* 4+3× ∧
VALUE	A name used without having been assigned a value	8×*X* *VALUE ERROR* 8×*X* ∧
INDEX	Improper indexing, e.g. an index using a negative number, a non-integer, or an integer larger than the size of an array	'*ABCD*'[5] *INDEX ERROR* '*ABCD*'[5] ∧
DOMAIN	A value outside of the domain of values used with a particular function	5÷0 *DOMAIN ERROR* 5÷0 ∧
LENGTH	The size (length) of one array does not match the size of the other array used with a function	2 3 × 2 3 4 *LENGTH ERROR* 2 3 × 2 3 4 ∧
DEFN	Improper attempt at defining or editing a program.	∇*A B C D* *DEFN ERROR* ∇*A B C D* ∧
CHARACTER	Improper formation of a character	;4 *CHARACTER ERROR* ;4 ∧
RANK	A function used with value(s) of the wrong rank	⍳4 5 6 *RANK ERROR* ⍳4 5 6 ∧
LABEL	Improper use of line labels in a program	∇*START* [1] *START*: *LABEL ERROR*
WS FULL	Workspace capacity too small to complete computation	(⍳1000)∘.×⍳1000 *WS FULL* (⍳1000)∘.×⍳1000

SUMMARY OF EDITING PROCEDURES

Editing procedures are used to define, refine, or change a program.

TYPE	NOTATION	EFFECT	EXAMPLE
General	∇ program name	Change from command execution mode to program definition mode.	∇*PROGRAM* [1]
Display	∇ program name [line number ⎕]	Display (line number) or Display whole program if (line number) is omitted.	∇*PROGRAM*[3⎕] or ∇*PROGRAM*[⎕]
Override	∇ program name [line number] (expression)	Replace an expression on a given (line number) with a new (expression) in program (name).	∇*PROGRAM*[5]*B*←1
Add	∇ program name	Add new line(s) on to a previously defined program (name).	∇*PROGRAM* [7]
Insert	∇ program name [decimal line number] (expression)	Insert a new line between (decimal line number) and (decimal line number) in program (name).	∇*PROGRAM*[2.5]
Delete	∇ program name [line number] [line number] ATTN	Remove (line) from program (name).	∇*PROGRAM*[4] [4] ATTN
Change Header	∇ program name [0](header)	Give program (name) a new(header).	∇*PROGRAM*[0]*NE*
Character	∇ program name [line number ⍞ (spaces)]	Prepare for changing specific characters on a (line) in a program (name) by displaying the line and spacing the type ball over a certain number of (spaces). Then / is used to strike out characters, and numbers insert spaces in front of characters.	∇*PROGRAM*[2⍞7]

LIST OF SYSTEM COMMANDS

A "system command" is used for workspace control and library management. (A library is a collection of workspaces.)

NOTATION	DEFINITION	EXAMPLE
)SAVE (work-space name)	Store the current (workspace) on disk memory. All programs and variables are saved.	*)SAVE MYWORK* *MYWORK SAVED* 07/08/77
)LOAD (work-space name)	Retrieve the (workspace) from disk memory to become the active workspace.	*)LOAD GAMES* *GAMES SAVED* 04/14/77
)COPY (library number) (work-space name) (program or variable names)	Copy particular (programs and/or variables) from a particular (workspace) in a particular (library) into the current active workspace.	*)COPY* 123456 *PLOT GRAPH*
)FNS	List alphabetically the names of all defined functions in the active workspace.	*)FNS* *GRAPH HANGMAN NIM MOVE*
)VARS	List alphabetically the names of all global variables in the active workspace.	*)VARS* *A B X Y*
)LIB	List the names of workspaces in user's library.	*)LIB* *MYWORK* *GAMES*
)WSID	Workspace Identification. Result is the name of the current active workspace	*)WSID* *GAMES*
)SI	State Indicator. Lists all suspended programs (including "pendant" programs which have yet to be completed due to the suspended programs) marked with astericks.	*)SI* *HANGMAN*[29] * *NIM*[3] * *MOVE*[1]
)CLEAR	Clear the active workspace.	*)CLEAR* *CLEAR*
)ERASE (program or variable names)	Remove a (program) or global (variable) from the active workspace.	*)ERASE GRAPH*
)DROP (work-space name)	Permanently remove the contents and name of a (work-space).	*)DROP MYWORK* *MYWORK DROPPED* 07/08/77

LIST OF SYSTEM VARIABLES

A "System variable" is a special variable which contains information relevant to the computing system and which may be used in APL expressions.

NOTATION	NAME	DEFINITION	EXAMPLE
⎕IO	Index Origin	Value is 0 or 1; used as the beginning of indices.	⎕IO←0 ⍳4 0 1 2 3 4
⎕PP	Printing Precision	Value is number of significant digits displayed in numerical output.	⎕PP←3 ○1 3.14
⎕PW	Printing Width	Value is the number of columns used in printing across the page/screen on a terminal.	⎕PW←10 ⍳9 1 2 3 4 5 6 7 8 9
⎕CT	Comparison Tolerance	Value is the number to which the difference of two numbers is compared in order to judge if they are equal.	⎕CT←.01 3.14=○1 1
⎕LX	Latent Expression	Value is vector of characters executed immediately (using ⍎) upon loading a workspace.	⎕LX←'''HI!''')SAVE MYWORK)LOAD MYWORK HI!
⎕RL	Random Link	Value is used by ? to generate random numbers.	⎕RL←16807 ?10 2
⎕AI	Accounting Information	Values are: identification # computer time, connect time, keying time (milliseconds).	⎕AI 123456 25 689200 8716
⎕LC	Line Counter	Values are statement numbers of programs being executed (esp. suspended programs).	⎕LC 18
⎕TS	Time Stamp	Values are: year, month, day, hour, minute, second, and millisecond of current time.	⎕TS 1977 12 24 23 59 59 9
⎕TT	Terminal Type	Value is: 1 - selectric; 2 - PTTC/BCD; 3 - 1050; 4 - 3270.	⎕TT 1
⎕UL	User Load	Value is the numbers of users currently on the (time-sharing) system.	⎕UL 23
⎕WA	Working Area	Value is the number of bytes of storage space remaining in the current active workspace.	⎕WA 32000

LIST OF SYSTEM FUNCTIONS

A "system function" is a special function which affects how the computing system performs and which may be executed in APL expressions.

NOTATION	NAME	DEFINITION	EXAMPLE
⎕CR	Canonical Representation	Result is literal matrix with rows of expressions from each line in a defined program, given as a (literal). ⎕CR (literal)	⎕CR 'AVERAGE' Z←AVERAGE N Z←(+/N)÷ρN
⎕FX	Fix	Result is defined program with expressions on each line from rows of a (literal matrix). ⎕FX (literal matrix)	⎕FX 2 11 ρ 'Z←AVERAGE N Z←(+/N)÷ρN '
⎕EX	Expunge	Result is erasure of program or local variable given as (literal) name. ⎕EX (literal)	⎕EX 'AVERAGE' 1
⎕NL	Name List	Result is vector list of first (n) names of labels (1), variables (2), or programs (3): (n) ⎕NL (1,2, or 3) or all names: ⎕NL (1,2, or 3)	1 ⎕NL 3 AVERAGE or ⎕NL AVERAGE
⎕NC	Name Class	Result is 0 if name is unused, 1 if used as a label, 2 as a variable, 3 as a program, 4 other. ⎕NC (name)	⎕NC 'AVERAGE' 3
⎕DL	Delay	Postpone execution a specified number of (seconds). ⎕DL (seconds)	⎕DL 60

Appendix

ANSWERS

Contents

U-PROGRAM 1

```
****************
```

Page 2

```
      'WITH SOME FOR YOU TO DO'
WITH SOME FOR YOU TO DO

      4 + 8
12
      7 - 3
4

      5 × 20
100

      100 ÷ 4
25
```

```
****************
```

Page 3

```
      2.5 + 7.1
9.6

      4 - 7
¯3

      3.0 × 5
15

      100 ÷ 3
33.33333333
```

```
****************
```

Page 4

```
      A - B
3

      A × B
130
```

```
****************
```

Page 5

```
      COUNTER
4

      COUNTER
5

      YEAR
2001
```

```
****************
```

Page 6

```
      SET
2   3   5   7

      SET - 1
1   2   4   6

      SET × 2
4   6   10   14
```

```
****************
```

Page 7

```
      SET + SIX
8   9   11   13   17

      SET , 6
2   3   5   7   11   6
```

```
****************
```

Page 8

```
      V × W
8   0   5   35   33

      W × V
8   0   5   35   33

      V , W
2   3   5   7   11   4   0   1   5   3

      W, V
4   0   1   5   3   2   3   5   7   11
```

```
****************
```

Page 9

```
      D , D , D , D
****

      D, E , S , I , G ; N , S
*ΔΔ*ΔOOΔO*Δ*Δ
```

```
****************
```

Page 10

```
      A , L , A
ABRACADABRA

      S , H , O , T
CURSE YOU, RED BARON!!!
```

```
****************
```

Page 11

```
      8 = 11
0

      12 = 12
1
```

```
****************
```

Page 12

```
      V < 5
1   0   1   1   0   1   0

      V ≤ 5
1   1   1   1   1   1   0
```

```
      V > 5
0  0  0  0  0  0  1

      V ≥ 5
0  1  0  0  1  0  1
```

****

Page 13

```
      4 ≠ 4
0

      4 ≠ 7
1

      '⎕' ≠ '⎕'
0

      '⌈' ≠ '⌊'
1

      'B' = 'ABBABA'
1  0  0  1  0  1

      'B' = 'ABBABA'
0  1  1  0  1  0
```

****

Page 14

```
      10 ⌈ 8
10

      12 ⌈ 8
12

      8 ⌈ 12
12
```

****

Page 15

```
      4 ⌊ 8
4

      12 ⌊ 8
8

      8 ⌊ 12
8

      P ⌊ Q
2  2  6  4  1

      Q ⌊ P
2  2  6  4  1

      Q ⌈ P
3  4  8  5  2
```

****

Page 16

```
      3 | 9 10 11
0  1  2

      4 | 4 5 6 7 8 9 10 11 12
0  1  2  3  0  1  2  3  0

      5 | ¯6 ¯4 ¯2 0 2 4 6
4  1  3  0  2  4  1
```

****

Page 18-Problems

```
      T + S
7.2  4

      'T + S'
T + S

      T - S
¯0.8  8

      T × S
12.8 ¯12

      T ÷ S
0.8  ¯3

      T , S
3.2  6  4  ¯2

      T = S
0  0

      T < S
1  0

      T > S
0  1

      T ≤ S
1  0

      T ≥ S
0  1

      T ≠ S
1  1

      T ⌈ S
4  6

      T ⌊ S
3.2  ¯2

      T | S
0.8  4
```

****

Page 20

```
      AREA

THE AREA IS
81
```

****

Page 21

```
      AREA

THE AREAS ARE
9  16  25  64
```

****

Page 22

```
      BASEBALL

THIS PROGRAM COMPUTES BATTING AVERAGE.
0.315
```

****

Page 23

```
      A

42
```

****

Page 24

```
      TRIANGLE

2  8  18  32  50
```

****

Page 25

```
      ⍳5

1  2  3  4  5

      ⍳3

1  2  3

      ⍳¯1

DOMAIN ERROR
      ⍳¯1
      ^

      ⍳3.5

DOMAIN ERROR
      ⍳3.5
      ^

      ⍳5 4
RANK ERROR
      ⍳ 5  4
      ^
```

****

Page 26

```
      V[3]

5

      V[5]

INDEX ERROR
      V[5]
      ^
```

****

Page 27

```
      W[2]

9

      W[3]

2

      W[2 + 3]

7

      W[2] + W[3]

11

      W[5.5]

DOMAIN ERROR
      W[5.5]
      ^

      W[6]

1
```

****

Page 28

```
      ⍴Y

8
```

```
      ρ'ABCD'
4

      ρSHAKESPEARE
24
```

****

Page 29

```
      L[1]
T

      L[2 4 1] , ' ' , L[1 4 3 5] , 'S'
RAT TAILS

      L
TWIST
      ρL
5
```

****

Page 30

```
      5 + 9 + 2 + 0 + 7 + 1
24

      +/ι9
45
```

****

Page 31

```
      SUM ÷ N
7

      SUM
21

      N
3
```

****

Page 32

```
      AVERAGE W
4

      W
5  9  2  0  7  1

      AVERAGE W
5
```

****

Page 34-Problems

```
      REVIEW
THE ANSWERS ARE
9
6
1  2  3  4  5  6  7  8  9
5
11
8
41
45
13
2  3  5  7  11  13
41
4
66
```

****

Page 36

```
      (6 × 4) + 5
29

      6 × (4 + 5)
54

      6 × 4 + 5
54

      6 + 4 × 5
26

      6 + (4 × 5)
26
```

****

Page 37

```
      (2 × 3 + 5 × 4) = (2 × (3 + (5 × 4)))
1

      Z1
9
```

****

Page 38

```
      T
2

      S
8

      R
3

      Q
9

      P
1  2  3  4  5  6  7  8  9
```

****

Page 39

```
      5 + 9 + 2 + 6 + 7 + 1
30

      5 + (9 + (2 + (6 + (7 + 1))))
30

      SUM
1

      SUM
8

      SUM
14

      SUM
16

      SUM
25

      SUM
30
```

****

Page 40

```
      5 × 9 × 2 × 6 × 7 × 1
3780

      MAX
7

      MAX
7
```

```
      MAX
7

      MAX
9

      MAX
9
```

****

Page 41

```
      ⌊/W
1

      MIN
1

      DIFF
6

      DIFF
0

      DIFF
2

      DIFF
7

      DIFF
¯2
```

****

Page 42

```
      -/ι6
¯3

      (+/S[1 3 5])-+/S[2 4 6]
¯3

      +/ι6
21

      -/ι6
¯3

      ×/ι6
720

      ÷/ι6
0.3125

      ⌈/ι6
6

      ⌊/ι6
1

      |/ι6
0
```

****

Page 43

```
      ι4
1  2  3  4

      2 × ι4
2  4  6  8

      ι4 × 2
1  2  3  4  5  6  7  8

      (ι4) × 2
2  4  6  8

      3 + 2 × ι4
5  7  9  11

      CENTIGRADE
10  20  30  40

      FAHRENHEIT
50  68  86  104
```

****

Page 45-Problems

```
      ιE
1  2  3  4

      I × ιE
2  4  6  8

      ιE × I
1  2  3  4  5  6  7  8

      (ιE) × I
2  4  6  8

      E + I × ιE
6  8  10  12

      +/E + I × ιE
36

      E + I × E - I
8

      (E + I) × E - I
12

      (E + I) × (E - I)
12

      +/V × W
179

      -/R < W
¯1

      (⌈/W) - ⌊/W
8

      (+/W) ÷ρW
5

      R ⌊ E ⌊ V ⌊ I ⌊ E ⌊ W
2  2  2  2  2  1

      ⌊/ R , E , V , I , E , W
1
```

Column 1:

****

Page 48

```
      1∧1
1
      1∧0
0
      0∧1
0
      0∧0
0
      1∨1
1
      1∨0
1
      0∨1
1
      0∨0
0
      ~1
0
      ~0
1
```

****

Page 49

```
      ~L ∧ K
0  1  1  1
      (~L) ∧ ~K
0  0  0  1
      +/~(L ∧ K) ∧ L ∨ ~L = K
3
```

Column 2:

****

Page 50

```
      ∧/K
0
      ∨/K
1
```

****

Page 51

```
      ∧/L ∨ K
0
      ∨/L ∧ K
1
```

****

Page 52

```
      Q × P
2  0  5  0  11  13  0  0
```

****

Page 53

```
      K / 6 2 8 4
6  8
      K / 'FLIP'
FI
      1 0 0 0 0 1 0 1 0 1 1 0 1 0 0 /'STOP THE RECORD'
STEREO
```

****

Page 54

```
      1 0 / 3 5
3
      0 1 / 3 5
5
      0 0 / 3 5
```

****

Page 55

```
      POW

4
16
64
256
```

****

Page 59

```
      POWOW

5
25
125
625
```

****

Page 62

```
      2 POWER 3

8
```

****

Page 65

```
      6 * 2

36

      7 8 9 10 * 1 2 3 4

7  64  729  10000

      3 × 3 × 3

27

      3 * 4

81

      3 × 3 × 3 × 3

81
```

****

Page 66

```
      9 * .5

3

      ¯16 * .5

DOMAIN ERROR
      ¯16*0.5
        ^

      ¯8 * 1 ÷ 3

¯2

      2 * ¯1

0.5

      0 * 0

1
```

****

Page 67

```
      AB 8

8

      AB ¯8

8

      ABS 11

11
```

****

Page 68

```
      |¯3 × ¯3

9

      |3 × ¯3

9
```

****

Page 69

```
      5 RES 13

3
```

****

Page 70

```
      5 RES 13

3

      5 | 13

3

      3.14 - 1 RES 3.14

3

      FLOOR 3.14

3

      CEILING 3.14

4
```

****

Page 71

```
      ⌊8.0 8.3 8.6 8.9 9.2 9.5

8  8  8  8  9  9

      ⌈8.0 8.3 8.6 8.9 9.2 9.5

8  9  9  9  10  10
```

****

Page 72

```
      ROUND 3.14

3

      ROUND 3.6

4

      ROUND ¯2.55

¯3

      ROUND ¯2.0904

¯2

      (10 * ¯4) × ⌊0.5 + X × 10 * 4

1.6667
```

****

Page 74-Problems

```
     0 0 0 0 1 1 0 0 0 0 0 1 1 1 1 0 0 0 0 0 0/'BEFORE YOU VIEW MORE,'
```

REVIEW

```
      (4 = 4) ∧ 5 = 5
1

      (3 ≥ 4) ∨ 5 ≠ 5
0

      (~∧/LOGICAL) = ∨/~LOGICAL
1

      2|+/LOGICAL
1

      2*+/LOGICAL
8

      |+/LOGICAL
3

      |-/LOGICAL
1

      ⎕←S←3
3

      ⎕←T←(S≠⍳S+1)/⍳S+1
1  2  4

      T * S
1  8  64

      S * T
3  9  81

      (S * 2) ⌈ 2 * S
9

      ((S+1) * 2) = (S * 2) + (2 × S) + 1
1

      (S××/S-T)*.5
DOMAIN ERROR
      (S××/S-T)*0.5
      ∧

      ⎕←P←2
2

      ⎕←X←20÷3
6.666666667

      (10*-P)×⌊.5+X×10*P
6.67

      ∇ OFF←X ROUND P
[1]     OFF←(10*-P)×⌊0.5+X×10*P
      ∇

      ∇Z←L MIN R
[1]   →(L<R)/4
[2]   Z←R
[3]   →0
[4]   Z←L∇

      TΔMIN←⍳4

      R←1.667 MIN 2
MIN[1] 4
MIN[4] 1.667

      S MIN R MAX T[S]
3
```

****

Page 78

```
      ?2
1

      ?52
40
```

****

Page 79

```
      ?6 6
3  4

      ROLL
3

      ROLL
10
```

****

Page 80

```
      ALPHABET[?ρALPHABET]
Y

      ALPHABET[?26 26 26 26]
JNVA
```

****

Page 82

```
      6 ∊ ι5
0

      2 ∊ ι5
1

      'B' ∊ VOWELS
0

      'COMPUTER' ∊ VOWELS
0 1 0 0 1 0 1 0
```

****

Page 83

```
      ∨/ 'LINGO' ∊ VOWELS
1

      VOWELCHECKER 'CONSONANTS'
1

      VOWELCHECKER 'WHYZZ'
0
```

****

Page 85

```
      4 ↑ W
5  9  2  6

      W = 6 ↑ W
1  1  1  1  1  1

      ¯3 ↑ W
6  7  1

      ¯5 ↑ W
9  2  6  7  1

      ¯8 ↑ W
0  0  5  9  2  6  7  1
```

****

Page 86

```
      3 ↓ W
6  7  1

      ¯4 ↓ W
5  9

      ¯6 ↓ W



      3 ↑ 'APLOMB'
APL

      TRI 'ANYTHING'
ANYTHING
NYTHING
YTHING
THING
HING
ING
NG
G
```

****

Page 88

```
      5 ? 5
5  2  1  4  3

      I
4  3  2  5  1

      2 ? 5
5  3

      3 ? 5
2  5  1

      5 ? 5
1  2  3  5  4
```

****

Page 89

```
      13 ? 52
16  5  12  37 46  13  31  17  11  1  27  48  43

      13 ? 13
4  3  13  10  11  1  6  9  2  12  7  5  8

      14 ? 13
DOMAIN ERROR
      14?13
        ∧
```

****

Page 90

```
      I
3 1 5 2 4

      ⎕ ← PER ← ⍳⍴I
1  2  3  4  5

      ⎕ ← PER ← PER[I]
3  1  5  2  4

      ⎕ ← PER ← PER[I]
5  3  4  1  2

      ⎕ ← PER ← PER[I]
4  5  2  3  1

      ⎕ ← PER ← PER[I]
2  4  1  5  3
```

****

Page 91

```
      ⍋D2
3  5  4  1  6  2

      D2[⍋D2]
¯2  0  2  6  7  9

      SORT V[(⍴V)?⍴V]
¯4  0  3.5  5  7  9  13.2
```

****

Page 92

```
      D2[⍒D2]
9  7  6  2  0  ¯2

      ⍒6 5 7 8 9
5 2 1 3 4

      S
TUNPEEN

      S[⍋N]
NEPTUNE

      S[⍋N]
NEPTUNE
```

****

Page 93

```
      ALPHABET ⍳ 'MAN'
13  1  14

      ALPHABET[18 15 2 9 14]
ROBIN

      1 + ⍴ALPHABET
27
```

****

Page 94

```
      LSORT 'SLOT'
LOST
```

****

Page 95

```
      ⍋6 9 ¯2 2 0 7
2  4  3  0  5  1

      ⍒6 9 ¯2 2 0 7
1  5  0  3  4  2

      ⍳8
1  2  3  4  5  6  7  8

      'ZERO'[2]
E
```

****

Page 98

```
      B
9

      N
34
```

****

Page 99

```
      5 × 8 ⌈ ⎕ + 2
⎕:
      7
45
```

****

Page 100

```
      B
ENTER

      C
ANY

      ρC
3

      B , C , A
ENTERANYLITERALS
```

****

Page 101

```
      X
ACETYLENE
```

****

Page 108

```
      END
VALUE ERROR
      END
      ^
```

****

Page 109

```
      DRILL
  14
× 75
----
⎕:
      1050
  46
× 53
----
⎕:
      2438
  22
× 5
----
⎕:
      110
  68
× 68
----
⎕:
      4624
  93
× 38
----
⎕:
      3534

CONGRATULATIONS! WOULD YOU LIKE 5 MORE?
ENTER  Y  FOR YES,  N  FOR NO.
YES
  52
× 83
----
⎕:
      STOP
```

****

Page 113

```
∇DRILL[18] →(∧/'YES'∊⍞)/1∇

      DRILL

  19
× 36
----

⎕:

      STOP
```

****

Page 116

```
      TEMPER
HOW DO YOU FEEL ABOUT ME?
⎕:
      8
⎕:
      6
⎕:
      4
⎕:
      →
```

****

Page 117

```
      ⍝NO LIMIT
```

****

Page 120

```
      3ρ5

5   5   5

      6ρ8  9  10

8   9   10   8   9   10

      3ρ8  9  10  11  12

8   9   10
```

****

Page 121

```
      3  5ρ2

  2   2   2   2   2
  2   2   2   2   2
  2   2   2   2   2

      2  5ρι10

   1    2    3    4    5
   6    7    8    9   10
```

****

Page 122

```
      3  3ρ1  0  0  0
 1  0  0
 0  1  0
 0  0  1
```

****

Page 123

```
      3ρ'*'

***

      7ρ'TOOT'

TOOTTOO

      3ρ'SEXTUPLE'

SEX

      12ρ'OH! '

OH! OH! OH!
```

****

Page 124

```
      2 30ρ'AND MILES TO GO BEFORE I SLEEP'

AND MILES TO GO BEFORE I SLEEP
AND MILES TO GO BEFORE I SLEEP

      6 30ρ'TO BE OR NOT'

TO
BE
OR
NOT
TO
BE

      L

GOOD
PLAY
BILL
```

****

Page 125

```
      ρ,M

12

      M×3

   3    6    9   12
  15   18   21   24
  27   30   33   36

      (,M) = (×/ρM)ρM

1
```

****

Page 126

```
      MATRIX

   9    5    0    6
   2    4   11    3
  16    8   20    7

      ρMATRIX

3   4

      ,MATRIX

9   5   0   6   2  4   11   3   16   8   20   7

      MATRIX-2

   7    3   ¯2    4
   0    2    9    1
  14    6   18    5

      6⌈MATRIX

   9    6    6    6
   6    6   11    6
  16    8   20    7

      MATRIX=3

0  0  0  0
0  0  0  1
0  0  0  0

      3∊MATRIX

1

      MATRIX∊3

0  0  0  0
0  0  0  1
0  0  0  0
```

****

Page 127

```
      MATRIX[3;2]

8

      MATRIX[3;]

16   8   20   7

      MATRIX[;2]

5   4   8
```

****

Page 128

```
      MATRIX[2;4  2  3]

3   4   1

      MATRIX[3  2  3;3]

20   11   20
```

```
      MATRIX[1 2 3;1 2 3] = MATRIX[2;2]

 0 0 0
 0 1 0
 0 0 0
```

```
      MATRIX[I[1];I[2]]

7
```

```
      MATRIX[;⍳I[2]] = MATRIX[⍳I[1];]

 1 1 1 1
 1 1 1 1
 1 1 1 1
```

****

Page 129

```
      +/MAT

6  15

      +⌿MAT

5 7 9

      +/,MAT

21
```

****

Page 130

```
      ×/MAT

6  120

      -⌿MAT

¯3 ¯3 ¯3

      (+/+/MAT) = -/-/MAT

0

      (1×3×5÷2×4×6) = ÷/,MAT

1
```

****

Page 131

```
      L⌿M

SOLD
OHIO

      K/M

SL
OI
FN
TE
```

****

Page 132

```
      3 ¯1↑MATE

E
E
L

      2 1↓MATE

AIL
```

****

Page 135

```
      3 RANDOM 7

DTLNFBR
RYJNVAB
NRAJBKR
```

****

Page 140

```
      ⌽'NOSLIW'
WILSON

      ⌽'DOCNOTEIDISSENTAFASTNEVERPREVENTSAFATNESSIDIETONCOD'
DOCNOTEIDISSENTAFASTNEVERPREVENTSAFATNESSIDIETONCOD

      ⌽⊖M
 12  11  10   9
  8   7   6   5
  4   3   2   1
```

****

Page 141

```
      (⍴M̲) = ⌽⍴M
1  1

      ⍉4 3⍴'FOEANDICELEN'
FAIL
ONCE
EDEN
```

****

Page 142

```
      (⍴R) = ⍴B
1
      ¯1⌽'TOPS'
STOP
```

****

Page 143

```
      2⌽M
  3   4   1   2
  7   8   5   6
 11  12   9  10

      ¯1⊖M
  9  10  11  12
  1   2   3   4
  5   6   7   8

      ¯2⌽1⊖⍉5 2⍴'UPCLEESAAP'
APPLE
SAUCE
```

****

Page 144

```
      2 3 ⌽ 2 5⍴'LESTA'
STALE
TALES
```

****

Page 145

```
      (⍉L̲) = 2 1⍉L̲
1 1 1 1 1 1 1 1
1 1 1 1 1 1 1 1
1 1 1 1 1 1 1 1
1 1 1 1 1 1 1 1
1 1 1 1 1 1 1 1

      (⍴L̲) = (⍴L)[2 1]
1  1
```

****

Page 146

```
      D[I] = SQ[I;I]
1

      (⍴D) = ⌊/⍴SQ
1

      1 1 ⍉ 3 3⍴'IRSNBAACM'
IBM
```

****

Page 147

```
      ⎕←L̲M̲←2 2⍴'∘⋆○●'
∘⋆
○●

      ⌽L̲M̲
⋆∘
●○

      ⊖L̲M̲
○●
∘⋆

      ⌽⊖L̲M̲
●○
⋆∘

      ⍉L̲M̲
∘○
⋆●

      ⌽⍉L̲M̲
○∘
●⋆
```

```
      ⍉⌽LM

*●
∘○

      ⌽⍉⌽LM

●*
○∘

      1 0 ⌽LM

*∘
○●

      0 1⊖LM

∘●
○*

      1 1 ⍉LM

∘●
```

****

Page 148

```
      X∘.×Y

   1    2    3    4    5
   2    4    6    8   10
   3    6    9   12   15
   4    8   12   16   20
```

****

Page 149

```
      ρY∘.*X

5  4

      X∘.⌊Y

  1  1  1  1  1
  1  2  2  2  2
  1  2  3  3  3
  1  2  3  4  4
```

****

Page 150

```
      (⍳10)∘.×⍳10

   1    2    3    4    5    6    7    8    9   10
   2    4    6    8   10   12   14   16   18   20
   3    6    9   12   15   18   21   24   27   30
   4    8   12   16   20   24   28   32   36   40
   5   10   15   20   25   30   35   40   45   50
   6   12   18   24   30   36   42   48   54   60
   7   14   21   28   35   42   49   56   63   70
   8   16   24   32   40   48   56   64   72   80
   9   18   27   36   45   54   63   72   81   90
  10   20   30   40   50   60   70   80   90  100
```

```
      (∨/~VEGETABLE)/'PEARS'

PEAS
```

****

Page 151

```
      +/10 4 × 3 2

38

      (+/V×M[;1]),+/V×M[;2]

60  84

      V+.⌈M

20 19
```

****

Page 152

```
      ∨/1 0 1 ∧ 0 0 1

1

      ∨/0 1 0 ∧ 0 0 1

0

      ∨/1 0 1 ∧ 0 0 1

1
```

****

Page 153

```
      (¯1↓ρM) , 1↓ρN

3  5

      +/M[1;] × N[;1]

110

      R[2;3] = +/M[2;]×N[;3]

1
```

****

Page 154

```
      ⎕ ← P ← 2 3 ρ 6 1 2 3 0 5

6  1  2
3  0  5

      ⎕ ← M ← 3 4 ρ ⍳12

  1   2   3   4
  5   6   7   8
  9  10  11  12

      ⎕ ← Q ← P +.× M

 29  38  47  56
 48  56  64  72

      ρQ

2  4
```

****

Page 156

```
      ⎕ ← M ← 3 4 ρ ⍳12

  1   2   3   4
  5   6   7   8
  9  10  11  12

      0,M

  0   1   2   3   4
  0   5   6   7   8
  0   9  10  11  12

      0⍪M

  0   0   0   0
  1   2   3   4
  5   6   7   8
  9  10  11  12
```

****

Page 157

```
      M,¯1 ¯2 ¯3

  1   2   3   4  ¯1
  5   6   7   8  ¯2
  9  10  11  12  ¯3

      M,[1]M

  1   2   3   4
  5   6   7   8
  9  10  11  12
  1   2   3   4
  5   6   7   8
  9  10  11  12
```

****

Page 158

```
      V,[.5]V

  2   3   5   7
  2   3   5   7


      ρV,[.5]V

2   4


      V,[1.5]V

2 2
3 3
5 5
7 7


      ρV,[1.5]V

4 2
```

****

Page 159

```
      ⎕←L←4 3ρ'ABCDEFGHIJKL'

ABC
DEF
GHI
JKL


      L,'*'

ABC*
DEF*
GHI*
JKL*


      '*'⍪L

***
ABC
DEF
GHI
JKL


      L,[1]L

ABC
DEF
GHI
JKL
ABC
DEF
GHI
JKL


      L,[2]L

ABCABC
DEFDEF
GHIGHI
JKLJKL


      L,[.5]L

ABC
DEF
GHI
JKL

ABC
DEF
GHI
JKL


      L,[1.5]L

ABC
ABC

DEF
DEF

GHI
GHI

JKL
JKL


      L,[2.5]L

AA
BB
CC

DD
EE
FF

GG
HH
II

JJ
KK
LL
```

****

Page 161

```
      ⎕←C←3 3ρ2 ¯1 5 1 2 1 4 0 ¯1

 2 ¯1  5
 1  2  1
 4  0 ¯1


      ⎕←B←13 0 11

13   0   11
```

****

Page 164

```
      +5
5

      -6
¯6

      V + W
0  0  0  0  0  0
```

****

Page 165

```
      - 0>¯5
¯1

      SIGNUM  B
1  ¯1  0  1  0  ¯1

      B × SIGNUM  B
3  4.2  0  5.8  0  9
```

****

Page 166

```
      ÷3
0.3333333333

      ÷10
0.1
```

****

Page 167

```
      2.718281828*1
2.718281828
```

****

Page 168

```
      ⍟*3
3

      (⍟N)÷⍟B
2

      B⍟N
2
```

****

Page 169

```
      10⍟10*2
2

      10⍟1000
3

      10⍟10000 100000 1000000 10
4  5  6  1

      7⍟7*3
3

      3⍟81
4
```

****

Page 170

```
      ○2
6.283185307
```

****

Page 171

```
      ⎕←RADIANS←○÷6÷⍳12
0.524  1.05  1.57  2.09  2.62  3.14  3.67  4.19  4.71  5.24
5.76  6.28
```

```
      3○RADIANS

0.577  1.73  5.73E15  ¯1.73   ¯0.577   ¯1.74E¯16 0.577   1.73
5.73E15  ¯1.73  ¯0.577  ¯3.49E¯16
```

****

Page 174

```
      DEGREES 60

1.05

      COSINE DEGREES 60

0.5

      (DEGREES 45)×360÷○2

45
```

****

Page 175

```
      RADIANS ○÷4

45

      30 = RADIANS DEGREES 30

1
```

****

Page 176

```
      X

3

      Y

1  2  3  4  5

      X MEMBER Y←2×Y

0

      'R' MEMBER 'WORD'

1
```

****

Page 177

```
      FAC 4

24

      FAC 0

1

      ×/⍳3

6

      ×/⍳4

24

      !5

120
```

****

Page 178

```
      !4 2

24  2

      !2.6

3.72

      2!8

28

      3!8

56

      8!3

0
```

****

Page 179

```
      2⊥1 0 1

5

      2⊥1 0 1 1 1

23
```

```
      (1×2*4) + (0×2*3) + (1×2*2) + (1×2*1) + 1×2*0
23

      (1×5*3) + (4×5*2) + (2×5*1) + 3×5*0
238
```

****

Page 180

```
      (8⊥2 4 7 3) - 8⊥2 4 6 3
8

      (8⊥2 4 7 3) - 8⊥2 3 7 3
64

      (8⊥2 4 7 3) - 8⊥1 1 1 1
754

      10⊥1 7 7 6
1776
      10⊥4 4 4
444
      10 10 10 10⊥1 7 7 6
1776
```

****

Page 181

```
      ⎕←R←W+.×B
3782

      ⎕←W←(×/1↓A),(×/2↓A),(×/3↓A),1
86400  3600  60  1

      1780 3 12⊥5 2 6
210

      24 60 60⊤3782
1  3  2
```

****

Page 182

```
      (4⍴10)⊤(4⍴10)⊥2 0 0 1
2  0  0  1

      2 2 2⊤4
1  0  0

       2 ⊤ 0
0
```

****

Page 183

```
      2 2 2⊤4 5 6 7 8
1  1  1  1  0
0  0  1  1  0
0  1  0  1  0

      (N⍴2)⊤(⍳2*N)-1
 0  0  0  0  1  1  1  1
 0  0  1  1  0  0  1  1
 0  1  0  1  0  1  0  1
```

****

Page 184

```
      TRUTH 2
 0  0
 0  1
 1  0
 1  1

      ⍴TRUTH 4
16  4
```

****

Page 185

```
      1780 3 12 DECODE 5 2 6
210

       1780 3 12  ENCODE  210
5 2 6
```

****

Page 186

```
      D
VALUE ERROR
      D
      ^

      '1 2 3 4 5' = ⍕⍳5
1 1 1 1 1 1 1 1 1
```

```
      (ρ⍎⍕⍳5) = ρ⍕⍎'⍳5'
0
```

****

Page 187

```
      2⍕⍳5
1.00 2.00 3.00 4.00 5.00

      ρV⍕A
10 30
```

****

Page 188

```
      (+/⍳1),(+/⍳2),(+/⍳3),(+/⍳4),(+/⍳5),(+/⍳6),(+/⍳7),(+/⍳8),(+/⍳9),+/⍳10
1 3 10 15 21 28 36 45 55

      |\⍳10
0 0 0 0 0 0 0 0 0 0

      ∨\0 0 1 0 1 1 0
0 0 1 1 1 1 1

      ∧\1 1 0 1 0 0 1
1 1 0 0 0 0 0
```

****

Page 189

```
      ρR
4

      +/Q
4

      (ρQ)=ρV
1

      L\'BACKSLASHOREXPAND'
BACK SLASH  OR  EXPAND
```

****

Page 190

```
      (12ρ1 0 0)\'APL\';(3ρ10)⊤212×30
A  P  L  \  3  6  0
```

Index

INDEX